Atlantis

THE AUTOBIOGRAPHY OF A SEARCH

Atlantis

THE AUTOBIOGRAPHY OF A SEARCH

ROBERT FERRO
AND
MICHAEL GRUMLEY

BELL PUBLISHING COMPANY · NEW YORK

All the events in this book are true, but some of the names have been changed for the sake of propriety.

517-117320
Copyright © MCMLXX by Robert Ferro & Michael Grumley
Library Of Congress Catalog Card Number: 71-116204
All rights reserved.
This edition is published by Bell Publishing Company
a division of Crown Publishers, Inc.
by arrangement with Doubleday & Company
d e f g h
Manufactured in the United States Of America

*For Margaret
and Marguerite*

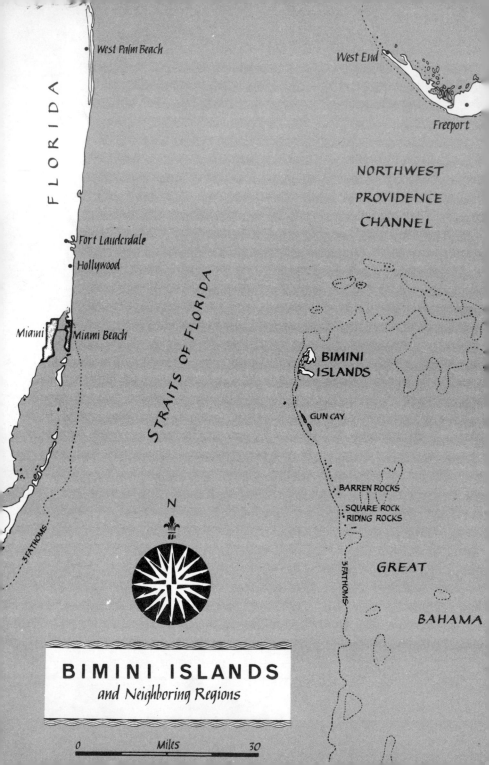

FLORIDA

West Palm Beach

West End

Freeport

NORTHWEST

PROVIDENCE

CHANNEL

Fort Lauderdale

Hollywood

STRAITS OF FLORIDA

Miami   Miami Beach

BIMINI
ISLANDS

GUN CAY

N

BARREN ROCKS

SQUARE ROCK
RIDING ROCKS

3 FATHOMS

GREAT

3 FATHOMS

BAHAMA

BIMINI ISLANDS
and Neighboring Regions

0   Miles   30

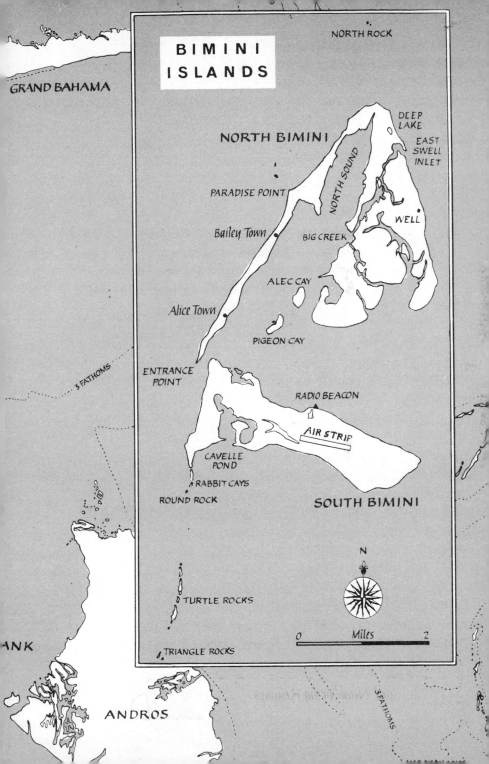

Falco told me, "I don't know exactly what has happened. I am the same person, yet I am no longer the same. Under the sea everything is . . . under the sea, everything is moral."

—JACQUES COUSTEAU
The Living Sea

Yaria, who told our fortunes in Rome, lived behind Piazza Barbarini with his mother. I don't know her name. She adored him much as a priestess would, as a phenomenon, special, and to be served; and she did her best to provide him with the comforts and attention she thought he deserved. She played the servant, though badly, in order that he might have a servant. As mystic, clairvoyant, and witch, he would otherwise never have been able to afford one.

She answered his telephone and door bell, took his appointments, kept his apartment, brought him tea, fluffed his pillows, and was so ineffectual in all of it that she amused him in the process. (The apartment had the look and sense of those cheap auction shops in Piazza Repubblica.) It was all her doing; he couldn't have been bothered.

She wore her clothes like an old woman, though she was barely sixty. She was abstracted and seemed dirty. Her lanky hair was yellow-gray, as were her eyes, which were fascinating. Since there was something waxy and unreal about her,

9

as if she had once sat rigid in a fortune teller's glass booth in a penny arcade, you were surprised that these yellow eyes could, as in a well-painted portrait, follow you about the room. She made me think of those savants one hears about who are inexplicably enlightened in some respect and terribly odd in all the rest; or of a child with a peculiar, terrifying yawn, during which, for one or two seconds, it jerks back its head or blinks open wide its eyes, the witness to something within itself that will eventually destroy it. But if she was crazy, she also had, at the least, panache, and, at the most, the genius of creative subconscious imagination. Michael might not agree, yet I think that all of Yaria's reckonings as medium depended on whether his mother was unique or merely insane.

Now she opens the door for us. She might be drugged. She keeps her eyes half closed. When she talks she looks sly rather than drowsy, and she looks at all things as if to her they hold equal value, person and post. Addressing Michael's chest and then mine, she tells us Yaria will be occupied for a while with some important clients who have arrived unexpectedly from Genoa. She says something also about dogs, cats, and an American lady.

Instinctively, I think, Michael and I know not to press her on any of it—we are inside the medium's house: the seance has begun. We are expected to wait, watch, learn, and pay when the time comes. This is the attitude which puts people in such good humor when they go to have their fortunes told. All sense of responsibility is gone. That and the fact that their egomania is about to be fed.

Yaria's mother shows us into a sitting room. No, it cannot be called a sitting room; it is tiny and contains only one small

*chair. The old lady's American woman is sitting in it, doing
a crossword puzzle. She introduces herself as Mrs. Lindholm,
and she speaks very little Italian.*

*I tell her Yaria doesn't speak any English. She smiles and
says she'll manage.*

*Yaria's mother imagines that the Signora Lindholm and
Michael have been given appointments for the same hour.
She blames her own mind for the mistake. Her mind has quite
gone, she says. She apologizes for a few moments and then
asks if we would mind waiting until Yaria can straighten
things out. A competition between Mrs. Lindholm and myself
has already begun but we say we don't mind. Mrs. Lindholm
goes on for a while about a train to Florence, but when she
realizes I am unimpressed she stops and goes back to her
crossword puzzle.*

*Yaria's mother has been watching us and listening atten-
tively to our English, a faint smile on her face, much like
a polite, deaf old lady at her grandchild's piano recital. Now
the smile fades and she is unnerved by the nature of the
silence between us all. Not only are there too few chairs to
go around, but now her guests are bored. She looks about her,
so obviously casting for an idea. Then the smile is back, and
she begins, slowly at first, as if testing the idea, and then with
charm and some gaiety because she has come up with a way
to amuse us while we wait; she begins to explain, one by
one, as many as time will permit, the hundred or so paintings
that are hung on or stacked against the walls of the narrow
room.*

*The paintings at first most strongly resembled store win-
dows done up in tempera and chalk for Hallowe'en. There
was that overdone, witch-on-a-broom quality about them,*

that same primitive flatness, awkward stiffness, and impossible angle of limb. Then, looking more closely, one thought of Hieronymus Bosch. We made the necessary complimentary noises. Very pleased, Yaria's mother went on.

"You, signora," she said to Mrs. Lindholm, "as a married lady, and most possibly a mother, you will appreciate this one. It's of me, the artist's mother." The painting was of a yellow-eyed cat. Suddenly then, I got a glimpse of the chasm which separated me from people like Yaria and his mother. I saw her in the back of a rocking gypsy wagon crossing a Hungarian border at night. "The cat. He calls me the cat." Mrs. Lindholm, not having understood a word, glanced up once, for her own reasons, and then went back to her puzzle. Her obliviousness seemed not to matter. I looked at Yaria's mother who stood with her head slightly back, looking at the painted cat, a canvas about two feet square and the best thing she had shown us so far. I said so.

"Yes, young man. I agree. It's very good. But look here." She pointed to what I had thought were romantic swirls of color in the background. They were figures. "This was a girl Yaria almost married. I never thought it a good idea, though I said nothing at the time. But her parents sent her away, to South America, where of course she died. And this is her mother, very aloof, the way most of these Romans are, the rich ones. It's charming in the young. But she's dead now. That's another story, yes . . ." She smiled and blinked her tired eyes. It was time to choose another painting. She leaned against the high bureau to one side, the parody of a statue in a garden, and looked about, at us, at the paintings. The flow had stopped perhaps and she was waiting on it. I lit a cigarette and waited with her.

Soon she had gotten herself together enough to pick an-

other painting, to muse over its surface and over the surface of her memories, her mind, as if the paintings were only an index to it all. I realized then that she was becoming very important to me.

The room was soon in great disorder. She had barricaded the door with paintings. Still she went on, rambling, randomly, as one does who browses down a list pronouncing only what catches the eye. There were long pauses, and sometimes she closed her eyes for seconds at a time. I listened much in the same way she talked, that is, absent-mindedly. She still had me, still led me, though I did not understand much of what she said. Michael seemed nearly asleep; no, he was off by himself in something. Mrs. Lindholm had given up completely and seemed utterly bored. Yaria's mother and I went on. I was sure she was taking me somewhere. But she was leading unaware of being followed, like a high-backed animal being tracked.

The idea came to me then, the answer, though I was still only vaguely aware I had been looking for one. But it appeared like land at sea: you were not even sure at first that it was there; perhaps you had gotten the whole thing wrong. But the idea was this: there was only one way out of the room—through the old woman's mind.

The idea was not baroque. Michael, Mrs. Lindholm and I were not trapped there, not in any sense that could conjure itself to me. It was simply between the woman and myself. I alone had the opportunity of leaving the room through a door that had no material existence. I could leave through the woman's words, through her dementia.

She had stopped talking altogether and was instead looking in turn at each of us, the way a lady does in a bus station. My impulse then was to feel sorry for her, because

13

she seemed, for the moment, pathetically lost. If she was psychic, she was unaware of it. If she had power or even a very keen intelligence, she used it inadvertently. But she was thoroughly at ease in this ambience. I do not mean her house. I mean that had I been ready to explain my idea to her she would have been unsurprised by it, and, in fact, ready to accept the possibility that she was leading me somewhere, though perhaps she would smile and quite innocently suggest we both wait and see what if anything we would be led to. I mean she might recognize herself as some sort of instrument.

She had borne a son, Yaria, who had a positive idea of his own uniqueness. It was she who had awakened that in him (if only by being strange herself). If she did not have what he, as a witch, claimed to have, then at least she was not foreign to it, not alien; she did not kill it. She inspired it, constantly. In a way, she had led him to that.

In my idea, she connected two rooms, or worlds. She was a means of passage between them, a corridor. I think she existed in that corridor always, and never fully emerged from it into either world.

I had tried to keep her in this room with me, to examine her, to classify and, I guess, explain her away. Now I wanted her to take me into that corridor, out of this room, to see if and where she could lead me. I was tired of this disrupted sitting room, this cluttered, scaled, and narrow room. I wanted to see the other, the huge, the high and empty huge room, so huge that only one corner of it would ever be perceived. So huge that beyond the dimness, in the darkness, the walls and the floor went out, without stopping, without meeting anything. They went on forever. Her mind had led you there. And when you looked up, the room would be filled with stars.

I

Fire

Our search for Atlantis was born in Rome, the city of Janus, god of beginnings. For Robert its midwife was the mother of a witch; its birth for him took place in the thin air of mind. For me, the birth was influenced by another sort of woman altogether. For me it began with a lady concerned with fire.

Before it became in America a substitute for martinis, a tranquilizer for the young, and an aphrodisiac for the old, marijuana was regarded by some as a key which, used respectfully, could unlock certain previously closed doorways of perception. It was, at the time of my first acquaintance with it, tied in with beatitude and the kind of subtle lode that separately Ferlinghetti and Salinger were mining. The impulse was to turn the music down rather than up and to tiptoe rather than crash through the tulip beds of one's sensitivities and emotions. Psychedelia was a means and not an end and the use of pot meant its utility. For some reason, perhaps because the mass media had not so completely shaped the separate nerve ends of the country into quite so homogeneous a clump, the use of pot was not yet a retreat but a rather special manner of advancement. Now, when we see ourselves as only pores on a sheet of anonymous national flesh, and now that our group traumata and catharses are infinitely more real to us than the lumps and pains of our individual lives, it seems quite natural that twisted Marx is no longer just a joke; opiates have indeed become the religion of the people. What seems to unite us is a quest for something to divide us, which makes for a dismal national congregation. Worshipers who are satisfied by only the wafer, the sugar cube, or the pipe, are obviously quite desperate to find some semblance of individual motive and purpose through their ingestion, and the rest of the service and the communion itself be damned.

But Rome. Though it is often raucous and though the pace is frenzied, one can always float above the language. And smoking, except perhaps on Via Veneto, is still in some quarters an art. One can formulate whole dreams and, more important, one can move toward them. Walking in the Forum or watching the slow yellow cats who live there sun in the crumbling corners of Largo Argentina, smelling the life and death of centuries in the damp alleys of Trastevere—by simply being alive in time, one feels specific. That glaze of desperation to be somehow Special (which Americans seem to carry about with their luggage) fades, and others' details no longer seem quite so threatening to one's own undetailed identity. One listens and stretches a bit and begins to move about on an extended plane of possibility. And, if one is very lucky, one meets someone like Raina.

She still believed that drugs were sacred and should be used with attention and careful appetite. She was a woman with dark hair and eyes, who looked vaguely as if she had once known Charlie Parker; she was introduced as a woman with a past as dark as her eyes. While we smoked and talked and walked in a group about Rome—there were seven of us, it was the night of the feast of San Giovanni—she told a long and convoluted fable concerning the beginnings of man. It drew from Thales and St. Peter, from the Koran and the Old Testament and from a great many ancient myths. It followed man's progress and his abuse of the powers of drugs. She believed her fable, and it was not difficult, listening to her, to share in that belief. It was easy to be charmed by her explanation that, whatever it was that grew on that tree in the Garden of Eden, it was not simply apples. And by her idea that the Garden itself was an experimental station, the first of its kind on earth, installed to explore the consequence of a non-earthly spirit or soul inhabiting an earthly body. Man was formed in the station as an experiment, and it was his capacity for expansion of the senses that made up the crux of the experiment. Raina believed more in dreams than in logic, and her explanation of an afterlife was that whatever one's imagination sowed, one's spirit reaped. The thread running through her fable was the necessity of opening up to stimuli of all sorts, of not categorizing good from evil, of responding positively in situations where the temptation would otherwise be to turn off response completely. Antennae, she said, were made for extending and not for retracting.

It was the meek, she said, those who avoided more than they responded to, who would inherit *only* the earth. Those with the courage to dream would inherit those dreams, dreams as infinite as the imagination.

She made these points and many more, hair falling about her eyes, teeth clicking, explaining. I listened to her, walking, all through the night, and after the sun had come up and we had separated I went to sleep and did some serious dreaming of my own.

I'd been keeping a journal of my dreams, and the night before I was introduced, by chance, to Raina, these had been two dream fragments:

"A nun sits on a bench, beside her there are one or two other park benches with other nuns. But around her head she is whirling or swinging some kind of cord with something heavy attached to it—perhaps a long knife—and warning me not to try to approach or sit down next to her. Or she will kill me. She and the other peripheral nuns all are wearing gray habits." And: "A man has come to speak with a political figure and I wait in the anteroom for his return. He comes out, red face flushed, and cackling with glee. He points to me and says that I'm to be the next Minister of the Treasury, while Robert is to be the next Minister of Churches. The head of whichever country it is reprimands the red-faced man for telling of the appointment so soon. He says something in reply, like, 'Everything's known instantly these days; it doesn't matter." Robert's head now slumps in either fatigue or faint."

I never know quite what dreams "mean." I've kept a dream-diary at separate times over a period of years and have yet to work out an accurate code to my own unconscious symbology. Our search for Atlantis was a series of smooth blunders from one point to the next on a psychic map. It is not that our eyes were particularly keen to these points, only that the points themselves were too large to be ignored.

The Spanish Steps in Rome, Piazza di Spagna, are at various times of the summer covered over completely with flowers. Each level is filled, from the top of the stone staircase, down both sides and meeting in the square before the fountain, extending down the lower flights and spilling nearly into the cobbled street. There are three displays.

The first is one of living flowers, coddled in separate gardens throughout Rome, spread out in the heaviness of full bloom. Plumerias, azaleas, and mimosa blossoms smear the steps with color, the greenery about the blossoms softens the background as German and American cameras click in a flurry of cinematographic greed. The flowers last for a week in the height of tourist season and when they are taken away there is a soft carpet on the steps of veined petals, dried and brown at the edges.

There are, then, paintings. Artists with tack-boards filled with press clippings sit or stand at various levels on the steps turning their canvases this way and that in the sun for buyers and tourists. The colors of the canvases are as brilliant as the flowers, and yet they too seem to fade until, at week's end, both they and their creators seem pressed and fragile and spent.

And then the true flowers of Rome appear, their faces the true canvases. Slumped or chattering, their gestures marked by both heightened nationality and sexuality, they reclaim the steps after the other displays have been cleared. The steps now move in waves of activity, a joke is passed like a sandwich among them and moves across and up through their brightly colored clumps. The "capelloni," the long-haired, the children. And the baby-hustlers, male and female, pouting, struck in attitudes of Caravaggio and Rafaello. And the budding drag-queens. Amid rustles of movement, and swoops of gesture and screeches of greeting, they pass the day. Chalk-white faces are hidden under sexless cloches, or eyes already wrinkled at the edges squint up at the sun. The network of living veins now is sometimes filled with chemical preservatives, the air ingested sometimes faint with hashish. Some veins are covered with tattoos, one occasionally with dainty white crescents at the wrist. But mostly, now, because it is the end of summer and the youth hostels across Europe are emptying, the arms and veins are innocent, and the vampires only huddle together in minority groupings, without prey.

Beside the Steps, and to the right, is the house where both Keats and Shelley lived, and where Keats died. There is a small memorial. (The bodies both lie in the English cemetery, close to the Pyramid in another part of Rome, behind low walls amid discreet cypresses.) Between this house and the Lord Byron Sweater Store is the Economy Book Center. Here all elements combine; both street people and tourists from the Hassler Hotel, transplanted Americans whiling away the time until the mail line forms at the American Express office at the end of the block. Here all books are in English and there is always a bargain table. In this shop, thanks to the private stock of one of its owners, we were introduced to works on the redoubtable Jeane Dixon, on the numerologist and palmist Cheiro, and to well-worn copies of various books on the "sleeping prophet," Edgar Cayce. It was during the time of the capelloni on the steps, the full heat of late summer, that we sat among the flowers and the faces and first looked into Cayce.

He was a man born in Kentucky in the 1870s who, after a short career as a stationery salesman, at the age of twenty-one, developed a type of constrictive paralysis of the throat muscles that made it extremely painful and nearly impossible for him to speak. Seeking help, he was unable to find any cure until as a last resort he persuaded a friend to induce in him the sort of trance-sleep he'd been able to enter as a child and in which he'd been able to absorb his grammar school lessons almost as if by direct osmosis. The friend's instrumentation was successful, and Cayce, in a voice restored by his trance state, was able to diagnose his own ailment and treatment so thoroughly that presently all signs of paralysis disappeared. Those physicians whom he'd consulted were intrigued by his recovery and its apparent cause, and, like a group of biology students at the dissecting board, proceeded to probe the possibilities of subsequent Cayce trances in order to cure their own patients. There were headlines and occasional court cases, and by the time Cayce died in 1945, there were also some fourteen thousand recorded trances prescribed for over eight thousand people.

The cases are called "readings" and they were recorded mainly by a secretary, Gladys Davis, whom Cayce employed through the years following his first prescriptive trance. These readings concern not only particular cures for particular physical ailments, they branch off into past lives and future earth-changes as well, touching down at various points on a calendar of time that stretches from 10,500,000 years ago to a time well into the twenty-second century. Cayce's sun sign was Pisces, and whatever questions of religious understanding he came up with in his trance state were filtered through a belief in the ideas and teachings of Jesus Christ. In his predictions of earth changes and in his recollections of past incarnations, there is always between the lines an affirmation of morality in accordance with the precepts of Christian love. And the readings themselves are the result of this impulse

23

toward sharing love and healing; all Cayce required to establish the particular ailments of a person were that person's name and location; there never occurs in the readings a sense of Cayce "hustling" his subjects, mainly because he never saw the majority of them.

What he said in his readings concerning Atlantis' "rise" is rather simple; that there would be signs of its existence, appearing in 1968 or 1969. In the bulk of his recorded readings this prediction seems rather an inconsequential afterthought, rather like the information that Jesus was fond of gerunds. It matters, of course, that the myth of Atlantis should be given validity, and it mattered probably to Cayce, but compared to all the information of what Atlantis was, a discovered temple or single artifact is no more "important" than a particular grammatical construction is to the over-all theory of a great theorist. But the idea of that undiscovered temple or single artifact, to me, when I first read of it, was for some reason tantalizing and delectable beyond measure.

(I do not know the first time the word Atlantis occurred to me. I remember drawing and coloring a cartoon in junior high school with a Miss Atlantis perched matter-of-factly among the other entrants in a Miss World contest. I thought it terrifically cute and sent it off to *Playboy*. They sent it back). Now, both Robert and I began to search out in the little bookstore anything pertaining to Atlantis. And there were arguments there. An American Lady with great spots of Howdy-Doody rouge upon her cheeks, overhearing one day our talk with the proprietors, launched herself on a hooting diatribe against Cayce and mysticism in general. The brunt of her attack was that he was conning a gullible public, and his readings were nothing more than the calculated pronouncements of a very good public relations man. It was when I grew in the passion of defense as red in the face as she, that I really felt the force of my own belief in whatever Cayce was and in whatever his readings represented. Until then psychic phenomena had been interesting, perhaps, but nothing to which I would affix the claws of my conviction. In the few minutes of that argument the concept of Atlantis became for me a fact.

Cayce's life and cases fascinated me. While his conscious religious specifications were not to my taste, still they acted as a framework, a vocabulary, upon which many otherwise unrelated subconscious messages could be hung. The waking, Christian, Cayce, and the sleeping prophet of wider scope depended on one another for more than vocabulary. The body they held in common needed a solid religious base to continue its work, while the mind in that body acted as a down-to-earth channel for the scudding clouds of far memory which continually crossed it. It seemed to me quite possible as I read, that, had he not been born a Christian, and completely accepted Christianity, Cayce would have gone mad. It was as if the world was contained in a bubble caption above his head, and was forever both revolving and evolving, and as if all the crises of mankind acted as pinpricks to the surface of such a spinning balloon.

The medical diagnoses effected by Cayce make up a body of fact so copious as to really preclude labels such as the Howdy-Doody lady's. The simple truth of the cures leads one in reading to entertain theories in the living-room of possibility which would otherwise never pass the stoop of derision. So it was with me. The business of dream interpretation was another inducement to relax whatever barriers of skepticism existed. The dream-diaries I had kept were kept more as a writer than a self-analyst, and were read more for images than for symbols, but the Cayce endorsement of such a recording made me feel that I was already tuned in to something more than mere creative masturbation.*

I had always thought of dreams as the smoke rising from the fire of experience. The Freudian line of dream-interpretation sometimes annoyed me because shape so often seemed the decisive factor in identifying symbols—but yet I would never have thought, before reading Cayce, that anything other than personal experience could form the symbols themselves. Neither would I have considered the possibility of past lives surfacing through dreams in the present.

* It is presumptuous, if not silly, to second-guess Cayce, but the following is an article which to me suggests a link between dreaming and health which may have occurred to him:

DOCTOR SAYS DREAM MAY AUGUR ILLNESS
(New York *Times*, *Aug. 20, 1969*)

"Dreams may be reliable forecasters of illness, according to a Soviet scientist, the magazine *Medical World News* reports. Reporting in the magazine *Ogonek*, Dr. Vasili Kasatkin says dreams may reflect a patient's sickness long in advance of a doctor's diagnosis. These are usually unpleasant and are related to the nature of the disorder, he says. As an example he cited a dream that a patient's chest got wedged while he crawled through a hole in a fence and said that this might portend pneumonia or pleurisy.

"Dr. Kasatkin found that the length of time between the dreams and the actual manifestation of illness varied. He said tuberculosis might give up to two months' notice, while delirium tremens might be signaled ten days in advance, and acute dysentery two days ahead.

"He said that some illnesses, such as bronchitis, influenza, and gastritis, might give only a one-day warning."

(The frustrating thing about recording and attempting to decipher one's own dreams, is the amount of "teasing" that occurs. While in New York City I dreamed recently of the Sistine Chapel, and felt myself sitting in, perhaps modeling, a Michelangelo pose. The next day whatever interpretation I worked out had to do with a desire to return to Rome, or else with some aspect of the modeling work I'd done. The obvious Christian religion aspect was also there. That night, turning on the scarcely used television, I was disturbed to see on the Late Show, Charlton Heston flat on his back with long-handled brushes. It seems to me teasing, I can't think of a better word, when whatever precognitive flashes I have are of no more use than the *TV Guide*.)

In the beginning of my larger understanding of what dreams and dreaming could be, I was lucky enough to have a dream that changed, if not my entire life, my entire focus on it, and direction.

Through the remainder of the summer in Rome, both Robert and I were working. Numerology was beginning to make a certain amount of sense to me, and I was attempting to correlate it with a code of color. I'd changed the way I signed my drawings, because of numerology, and was having a bit of success with them.

Also there was movie work. On the set of a film tentatively called *At Any Price,* at the De Paolis Studios in Rome, there were a great many Americans working as bit players who were otherwise legitimate, if unknown, bassos and contraltos, sculptors and painters. Between takes, in a mock-up of a Las Vegas casino, hundreds of elaborately done up Californians and Midwesterners moved cautiously between fake slot machines and roulette wheels. Between denunciations of the Guatemalan casting director and trashy stories about the female lead, there was a great deal of talk about California sinking into the sea, Cayce predictions, and other matters occult. It was the kind of atmosphere—a hot set, long hours on it, and little enthusiasm for the work at hand—which led to a real thirst for any kind of titillation. Crowd scenes were shot and reshot, the principals moving sluggishly through their paces while the extras sleep-walked around and around them. One of the Italian extras, a woman in her forties, was suddenly ejected from the set in an explosion of curses from the assistant director. She had managed, at every take, to maneuver her way from whatever obscure position the director had placed her in to a spot within six feet of the cameras, her eyes shining and lips parted. In her flurry toward the camera she resembled nothing so much as a great black moth drawn to its light. Ordered to leave, she became first incredulous, then resolute; two matrons and a grip were needed to carry her away. As she was being so removed, the word spread across the set that she was a witch. It was the perfect audience for such a rumor; the word was received and circulated with relish. A mild hysteria set in. The casino set, as large as a football field and crammed with five hundred people hemmed in by a jangle of movie machinery and pre-recorded noise, gave off little shudders of vaguely masochistic anxiety as the next scene was set. John Cassavetes was to detonate a small bomb, which in the film would cause the casino to be consumed in flames. Sound men and electricians now mumbled countercurses as they worked, and the five doors which were to be used as exits, should the bogus explosion become more than Special Effects, were clearly marked. We all took our places and waited through two false starts for the definitive scene.

Later, there was an official explanation concerning faulty

wiring, or inadequate insulation; salaries were held up for weeks and the producers hurled accusations at one another. What happened in the six minutes between the director's call of *"silencio"* and the heavy groan of the studio roof falling in upon itself was a scene of genuine mayhem. As the "fake" bomb spread flames from one end of the casino canopy to the other, and as the plastic and papier-mâché walls caught fire, simulated shrieks became cries of very real terror. The exits jammed as costumed croupiers and dowagers pressed through them and out into the fresh air. Miraculously, truly miraculously, there were no deaths. The cameramen wept over their destroyed footage and melted cameras, the director was taken immediately to the hospital, suffering from nervous collapse, and the studio and the building which housed it were completely destroyed.

The lady accused of witchcraft was more pathetic than sinister and the words she screamed while she was being led away actually concerned her previous screen credits and not maledictions upon the film or company. And yet she, in her own way, caused the fire. She caused it by reinforcing the mood of the crowd to such a degree that some kind of supposed retribution was inevitable. In a chain of causation, she perhaps addled the brain that shook the hand that placed the fuse that missed the wire that connected the powder which ought to have put out the really quite small explosion flash. Or she numbed the foot that kicked the cord . . . or she excited the fingers . . . or she did any of a number of things to a number of people because of what they felt or thought about her, things that resulted in the holocaust which occurred.

Such causation is hardly verifiable by what we think of as the scientific method. Such things as Intensity Quotients, and Rates of Subconscious Force, are not measurable quantities on any kind of scientific graph, and to try and analyze them in purely scientific terms would be ludicrous. They simply don't fit into the existing vocabulary. But I do believe there are laws which govern them, and thresholds beyond which there is no altering their direction.

On a much smaller scale but with some of these same laws working, I believe my particular dream of Atlantis was caused, or allowed, by my desire to have such a dream. It occurred during a period of time when I was opened up to a fairly wide spectrum of ego-reinforcing stimuli, and was therefore more inclined, as Robert sometimes says, "to feast on myself." The last two weeks in September were filled with activity; I had opened a show of my drawings at Galleria 88 and was in and out of Via Margutta almost daily because of it, also I was going through final auditions for a rather good part in a Napoleonic epic being filmed at Cinecitta. Robert's parents stopped in Rome for a week and then he and they spent another week with relatives in the south. On Monday of that last week I had this dream:

> I am standing in what appears to be a council or throne room, one of a group of about a dozen people. I seem to be an adviser or attendant to the female ruler, a woman in her forties or fifties, a priestess with fine classic features and silver-gold hair. She wears a long robe, and her eyes seem to see everywhere at once. There is no conversation in the room, all communication is made without speech, by some manner of thought telepathy. It is as if we are all controlled by this network of interlocking thoughts, held in ordered place by its telepathic web. The room has a stone floor and there is a large prism. I am standing to the left of the woman, the priestess, and the rest of the people

are spaced around her in a semicircle. One of these people, a fool or jester, or stranger, suddenly confronts the priestess with a toy pistol, or water gun, and pulls the trigger. Immediately the thought-network is relaxed and I experience the most exhilarating sense of freedom. It is overpowering—the relaxation of control affects all of us as the priestess is, for a brief moment, surprised by the toy gun which squirts out a long strip of colored paper instead of bullets or liquid. In that moment of freedom all I can do is fall to the ground, the stone floor, like an animal and begin to bay loudly. I see myself rolling on the floor, howling, but can do nothing to stop myself.

And, in another fragment,

now, outside the throne room, in a corridor or outer hallway, beside or behind large square-edged pillars of blue and white. The pattern on the pillars is rather simply and largely wrought, there are no other colors but blue and white. Another man and I seem to be waiting for someone or something, we seem to be hiding. I am, most definitely, in Atlantis.

The dream was vivid enough so that I wrote it out the next morning and sent it off to an actor-astrologer I had known in New York when I lived there. We had kept in contact over the years since I'd been out of the city, during that time he had been getting deeper and deeper into astrology; his last letters happily announced that he was finally supporting himself from astrology and no longer had time for acting. As I grew more and more interested in Cayce and the occult, my letters to him grew more numerous; now as I wrote out my dream I am sure my face wore a look of silly delight, such as a student's who has at last done a lesson that he knows will please the teacher. The best teachers seem never to be outdone by their pupils, however, and before reading my dream, Richard had written me this account of one of his own:

That night I had one of the clearest dreams I've ever remembered and was instantly aware that I was in Atlantis. I was in a room all of a clear substance that allowed the sunlight to come right through the walls. The floor also was clear. There were other women in the room all dressed in variations on a one-piece gown in different colors but I had distinct knowledge that the material of the gown was living and was respected as such. There was no furniture but some appeared to be sitting and others moving through space and not on the floor at all as if by some anti-gravity. There was a hole in the center of the ceiling and the walls of the building acted as a prism focusing sunlight (much more intense than any we know) onto another prism in the center of the room, stationary but not supported by anything. More or less floating. This was treated by all with great veneration and none went too close. We communicated freely but never spoke. It was all by thoughts. We each wore the snake circlet around head and arms usually seen in Egyptian art and had the bare breasts of the Minoans. We had a sort of high clog on our feet, which seemed to have some sort of function I couldn't figure out but looked like those that the Aztecs wore. The meeting was a conference of the greatest importance as we knew in various ways that our land was doomed. Suspended in the air in front of each of us were maps of the world as it was then, quite different in many respects. The maps were exact miniatures of the lands in question, even to each hill and river and tree, but, strange to tell, the maps were alive. The minute trees were growing, the little rivers flowing, and tiny waves beat on the coasts. We passed our hands over the maps to find proper places for the settlement of our people. I remember we did not look at the maps but at the prism and passed our fingers over the contours of the map. My fingers found the Nile Valley and an area in the eastern Mediterranean centered on Crete which is no more. Other things also occurred, but I will not mention all here. What do you think?

What I thought, when I read Richard's dream—which had occurred very nearly the same time as mine—was that, somehow, we had both been handed the same script. Robert returned with his parents on Thursday of that week and, while unpacking, casually mentioned that his father had, out of the blue, suggested that he take his boat down to the Caribbean for the winter. Robert saw the offer as an inducement to get him back to the U.S., and closer to his family— and found it amusing that his family would go to such lengths.

A little over a month before, an article had appeared in the Rome *Daily American* headed "Atlantis May Have Been Found." Now I took it out from the folder into which I had stuck it, and showed it to Robert.

Miami, Fla.: A noted archaeologist reported yesterday a "most exciting and disturbing?" discovery in Bahamian waters, of an ancient "temple" he said might be part of the legendary lost continent of Atlantis.

The mysterious find in six feet of water off a Bahamian island is the "first of its kind in the western hemisphere" said the archaeologist, Dr. Manson Valentine, one-time zoology professor at Yale University.

"The top is about two feet above the ocean floor," said Valentine, who inspected the "temple" for the first time last weekend. "The walls are sloping. I dug into the sand and managed to feel about another three feet down. It is obviously much deeper, but we will not know much until we excavate. The material is a kind of masonry and it is definitely man-made."

Valentine said he has hopes the "temple" might be part of Atlantis, the ancient lost continent which, legend has it, vanished beneath the sea after a mighty cataclysm.

Robert read the article, and then continued unpacking his shirts and underwear. What for me was a moment of high drama and excitement seemed to be for him only a passing parenthesis. I felt that I was being thrust onto the stage of a terribly important piece of theater, whereas he wasn't even aware that he had been cast. I brought out my dream. I brought out Richard's. Finally, reluctantly, he began to see things coalescing.

We had both read Cayce's prediction that signs of Atlantis would appear in the Bahamas, probably off Bimini, in either 1968 or 1969. We had been interested, I probably slightly more than Robert, in what form these signs would take, and in what type of impact they would create. But thus far, until his father had so blithely and unwittingly, knowing nothing of our interest in the area, dropped the suggestion of a winter cruise, neither Robert nor I had been more than objectively enthusiastic. There we were, rather comfortably set up in Rome, in an atmosphere of agreeable stimulation for all the work we were doing, suddenly contemplating a break with all the associations, both professional and social, that we had made. And thinking about taking a boat, about which we had not a shred of knowledge, into an area we knew absolutely nothing about, in the hopes of finding some remnant of a civilization which hadn't been heard from for eleven and a half thousand years. It is no small wonder that our friends thought the idea quixotic at best, and, at worst, the very zenith of lunacy.

It seems all we ever really want to know is the beginning. Of everything. We catapult ourselves further and further back through history and possibility until we reach the point beyond which there is no trace of communication or culture. That is the point then, for our particular minds, which signifies effect rather than cause, which represents the first segment of the "end." There, behind that point, is the gulf of silence, the invisible smile on the face of an unknown God.

Robert Ardrey and Arthur Clarke have taken us, by various methods, a long way back to a dark corner of the zoo. There, split skulls and jawbones line the cage floor, and the glint in the resident hominid's eye is one of canny territoriality. There we are, hairy in the Pleistocene. A shaft of light, a coincidence of matter, causes an aggressive sizzling in our ancestral brain-pan and from that moment on, we are men. If we accept this moment, we accept it as a beginning. But it is not The beginning: what we now concern ourselves with is that shaft of light. And when somehow, by theory and invention, we manage to explain that shaft, our imagination comes up against the inverted mirror of time itself reflecting seconds and minutes on the clock-dial of space. The answers to small riddles seem always to raise enormous questions. We find, as we tumble backward in possibility, that the very concepts of "beginning" and "cause" are useless. As space-geography and earth-philosophy blend, the science of astrology attracts more and more interest, stretching as it does questions of physical morality into a realm of heretofore purely spiritual influence. If, through astrology, the smile on the face of that unknown god becomes visible, with every crease and wrinkle somehow explainable, we still are unable to see the hand which painted the smile in the first place. The most important aspect of our space-discoveries is that they give us no choice but to admit our complete lack of understanding and knowledge about why we are on *this* planet. We have moved, through the last few centuries on earth, from a period of smug, if terrified, anthrocentricity during the Middle Ages, into an era of comprehension which makes man no more than a footnote in an encyclopedia of possibility, an encyclopedia shelved with a million others in the library of an eternal universe.

We no longer think of mankind as the pivot on which the stars all swing. The more we become aware of and face the inadequacies of our species, the greater should be our willingness to believe in, even hope for, the possibility of some other form of life on some other cosmic plane. It becomes increasingly clear that, as supposed rulers of our galaxy we are shabby figures indeed, understanding so little and proclaiming so much, presuming to unite the planets with our influence while here on earth we display as much fellow-feeling as a bowl of hungry guppies.

Our first thrust to the moon was sweet, even considering the sometimes nearly pathetic amount of national back-slapping that accompanied it (Walter Cronkite wondering how the under-privileged and disaffected could possibly feel either way with the American flag at last stuck in the Sea of Tranquility; Richard Nixon's too-spontaneous summing-up —that it, the day of the moon-landing, was the most important day since the Creation). The event itself was tremendously exciting; the competitive enthusiasm, the back-slapping, made believable the Lorenz-Ardrey theory of space-racism as well-channeled territorial aggression. As a substitute for war, dancing on the moon is attractive. (As a substitute for peace, however, it is not.)

Acceptance of Cayce's Atlantis is acceptance of the idea that we have come this way before. Not, perhaps, that we, as our own Atlantean ancestors, ever reached the moon and stars, but that we destroyed ourselves and our culture because of a misuse of solar or nuclear power. In the readings on file at Virginia Beach, Cayce explains that the last of the three cataclysms which destroyed the culture of Atlantis came about through an upsetting of the natural balance. This balance was thrown off by either nuclear blasting or some other manner of touching off subterranean explosion and earthquake. The combination of natural disaster and either human error or malice occurred, according to the readings, for the last time in 9500 B.C. There had been two previous explosions, earthquakes, or floods, which occurred much earlier in Atlantean time, causing the breaking up of the original land mass into five smaller islands. Whatever were the particular reasons for these eruptions and subsequent cataclysms, the general effects were all-consuming. The destruction was so complete as to virtually wipe clean the slate of human endeavor and culture, erasing by fire and water all that had been of the physical civilization. There are echoes, in the civilizations of Egypt, Crete, and South and Central America, of what the Atlantean culture might have been, but there have been no artifacts or archaeologically acceptable relics found which would explain and prove to this, the present age, the validity of that one. The Atlantean Age has no rooms devoted to its crafts and clothing styles at the Metropolitan Museum, and there is no existing biograph compiled by an Atlantean Margaret Mead.

There is, so far as we know, only Plato. And even he,

that most specific and beautiful of writers, is thought to have indulged himself with metaphoric fantasy in writing the dialogues, the *Timaeus* and the *Critias*. There are giggles in the cloakroom of nearly every scientific hall where the subject of Atlantology is broached. It is sure death for any academician to become even peripherally involved with the question of its existence. The network of proof, therefore, is not one of established scientific methods, and those who engage in the attempt at proof are never those with advanced degrees in Prudence or Practicality.

Atlantis is a dream and, for many, whether or not there is substance behind the dream is a question of minute importance. Atlantis represents so much to so many that a unified explanation of its importance is impossible; its very open-endedness is in many areas its appeal. Either the road to its acceptance is a rainbow, and its golden towers are woven of cotton candy, or, it is the certain base for all Aztec, Olmec, and Mayan cultures with concrete dates of existence and a symbology which unites particular civilization of a specific place and time. Atlantis is all that man might have become, mixed in with all that he is today.

In terms of reincarnation, those who lived in Atlantis are said to have possessed the first souls. Souls had been combined with animal forms, and the mixture produced sometimes brilliant, sometimes grotesque results. These souls, once incarnated into earth-life, became locked into particular earth-forms, and so lived out lives within their first earthly bodies. And when these bodies died, the souls were freed to choose again the vehicles which they would ride through another life-span and which would afford them the necessary opportunities for self-perfection. Perhaps, for some, one time around was quite enough. Perhaps, because they were the very first, these souls had a far different scorecard in terms of self-perfection than the ones we carry around with us today. But each time back, a particular soul combined more and more elements and the scoring became more and more sophisticated until what would once have been an improvement became a degradation of itself, and no one but itself could really know the proper moral code to follow. This combining and refracting of characteristics would seem to have produced early on in the process subtleties of good and evil which would take hundreds of centuries to work out. The soul-memories which were produced in that early age now necessarily stretch back over a period much longer than recorded history, these memories are the networks within each soul where the tallies are kept, and which provide the dappled passageway upon which present minds may travel in quest of an otherwise irretrievable past.

These memories, too, are factors which lead many people in the present to believe that skills and tastes acquired in one incarnation show up in subsequent lives, and that our present highly technological age owes as much to the achievements of an ancient past as to the pooled scientific knowledge of the present. That is, many people—Cayce among them—believe that we have quite literally passed this way, achieved this pinnacle of technical advancement, once before.

It is always possible that, vast as the span of our earth's existence seems to us, that existence may be even vaster; earth may be twice or ten times as old as we believe it to be, and this last period of history which we think of as the total span may be only a portion of its life. Assuming that this is at least possible, there may have been epochs and entire lines of evolution which, at the end of their particular track, burned themselves up, and out. And left not a trace, not a bobby pin or laser gun slowly rusting in what would be called by the succeeding menagerie its own pre-Cambrian sludge.

With the Age of Aquarius at last upon us, it may be that it is our time to decide whether, as a species, we will go any further. The implications of Aquarius are that men ought to be able, by now, to control each their own life and particular destiny, that we ought to have, by now, enough knowledge of our own particular recurring souls to exist without the strictures of any moral code but that which those souls softly dictate. The alternative is, of course, oblivion. The Age of Aquarius may be the moment of evolutionary truth for this stage of earth-life, that time which we have been crawling toward since Cancer-in-the-mud.

If this is true, and if we, as twentieth-century human beings, are simply the outer ripple in the splash of a rock thrown again and again into the pool of time, then it seems well to consider the possible nature of the pool itself. Though we have relinquished our central position belief, and have reluctantly come to accept, through the ages, the fact that we are incidental to both space and time, we have not yet come to the point where we can, with any measure of species-sanity, give up our hope of heaven. That hope is so comfortably finite. We die, and go Somewhere Else, and never again involve ourselves with the details of creating and conducting our own existences. Once we make that big leap, we will be forever cradled and comforted in the palm of a cloudy hand. The Age of Pisces, the Age of Christianity perhaps, gave us that hope. It seemed to be what we needed at the time, it promised a cushy reward for those who refrained from tearing themselves and each other apart here on earth. But now, inasmuch as we have managed, not prettily and certainly not with special honors, to wade through these last two thousand years, we are faced with the next giant step, the next segment of the wheel. Now, in order to continue at all, we must stop merely swimming in the pool and begin to regulate the water.

To know what it is to be a human being is to begin to know what separates soul from spirit and spirit from flesh. And to begin to take responsibility for the action of the flesh. Somewhere between Christian fatalism and psychoanalytical insight—both of which are forms of accepting extraneous currents, rather than being guided by that line of behavior which is particularly and exclusively one's own—there ought to be an attitude in consciousness which accepts reincarnation. There is nothing in Christian doctrine which denies the concept of reincarnation, but it is largely incorporated into other dogma and so absorbed. The church held the world together for a great many years, now that it can no longer do so it is disintegrating. Yet many of the principles of karma are contained in Western theology, and Christianity has, sometimes inadvertently, passed these along. The hope of heaven was a necessary hope for a large segment of mankind when an acceptance of reincarnation would have been impossible. We were all a great deal younger in the Dark and Middle Ages and there's no telling what we would have done with "bad karma" as an excuse. Christianity itself was used often enough as a toy and a weapon, reincarnation could have been self-defeating.

(In Bettendorf, Iowa, where I was a child, I remember a girl name Jan Devine loaning me a book concerning reincarnation. I was perhaps a freshman in high school at the time, in the middle of the midwestern middle class, and was more puzzled than pleased with the book. How or why she became interested in it I never knew, but she was both attractive and intelligent and so I looked into it. I gave back the book in study hall, rather furtively and in the hope that she wouldn't say anything more about it. She didn't, and I never mentioned anything about what seemed to me a totally useless, if not completely whacky, idea. It appealed to me on no level whatsoever and I remember not a word of whatever I read. If, somehow, I could have used it to enhance my popularity, or to push me from second-string into first position right-guard on the football team, or even somehow to facilitate learning and memorizing the first fifteen lines of *Thanatopsis,* then I might have retained some of it. The circumstances of my own evolution were not right, however, until ten or so years later in Rome when another attractive and intelligent young lady loaned me books on both Cayce's and Gina Cerminara's theories of reincarnation. Between Miss Devine and Miss Pamper there had been a lot of empty time.)

Now the time gives none of us a great deal of choice; we have thirty years to take a crash course in Personal Humanity, and we either pass, into the Aquarian Age in harmony with it, or we fail, and as a species, die. Our souls need bodies to slip back into, not cadavers with bones of putty, and not the stillborn grotesques that radiation produces. By killing, we kill reason. And by killing reason, we kill the opportunity for another time around.

If Atlantis existed as Cayce and Plato describe it, then its final cataclysm was the result of some kind of colossal mistake. For the degree of advancement it attained to be so completely destroyed indicates that, whatever the creative forces shaping the culture, there must have been equally potent destructive forces. Man's recorded history is written in such dichotomies, in all probability his unrecorded drama contains the same competing elements. Further, it is not a terribly bad bet to make that Atlantis' schizoid last years may not have been a great deal different from our own. It is possible that their technology took other forms and was used for different ends than our own, it is possible that it existed concurrently with other forms of evolving primates. The possibilities are endless. I believe, but it is only my particular surmising, that our level of civilization will not approach the peak that theirs did until we are well into Aquarius. And just because we make it that far doesn't mean, astrologically or otherwise, that our infinite perpetration into the future is assured.

There is also another possibility. The Atlantean culture may have reached its peak, and then, not being able to stretch its civilization further, it may have simply vanished. The volcanoes and the tidal waves may have been excuses for posterity, and the destruction only the means to a fast getaway. A getaway from a planet which had for a time offered up the last of its usefulness, would needs be furnished with such theatrical effects. The idea of such a getaway is to me intriguing, even more so are the various locations for cosmic hideouts. Is it not possible that Atlantean souls who reached their perfection as the exodus began, are, even now, giggling at our knitted brows from where they bask on the beaches of Titan, from where they unpack picnic hampers in the crystal fields of Pluto?

On the cruise ship *Cristoforo Colombo*, on a trip between Algeciras and Naples, Robert and I met a remarkable Englishwoman who delighted us with anecdotes about Ruth Draper, the English class structure, and various interrelated stories about her experiences at sea and her life in Oxford. When the ship docked in Naples, the three of us took the train up to Rome together, where she was going to look in on her son and his wife who were there writing theses and film criticism. Through her we became friendly with her son and daughter-in-law. I taking Italian from Geoffrey, Robert engaging in heated arguments with Rosalind over things political and literary. Our apartments were located not far from one another and we saw each other a good bit in the open market, in and out among the chicken and fruit stalls. A close Italian Communist friend of theirs dropped in one day en route from Cuba to Paris, somewhat disquieting tea and conjugations, with some articles he had written for various periodicals. He passed through in rather a flurry, but dropped the name of Josephine Hawke, his agent in Milan who, he said, would be very interesting in my drawings. She turned out to be more interesting than interested, appearing one morning with the drawings I'd sent her, much enthusiasm, and the chicest maxi outfit I had ever seen. Later her rouged nipples and feather boa were to create a great deal of excitement in Positano, but this was winter, and Rome. It was finally through Josephine, from Auckland, New Zealand, writer, agent, and model, that we were introduced to Jacinto Yaria, mystic, painter, and witch.

Yaria's fingers, in my mind, seem always about to stroke a cat. The features of his long face seem equally drawn out in one long, down-sloping curve. He is a slight man, and the tiny room in which he sits, reading palms and Tarot cards, seems well suited to his size, if not to ours as we sit slightly scrunched on a low couch under a low ceiling. He has dismissed Mrs. Lindholm, the lady with a conflicting appointment, and now his mother is left alone in the anteroom, while we three settle down to serious questions of the future. We mention Josephine's name, he inquires after her health, we say she is well and will no doubt be calling on him soon, then he asks us, first one and then the other, to see our hands.

This palm reading didn't take much time, there were questions in my mind about career conflicts—it was by then a week into October—other galleries and the movie part still hovered, and my novel was moving rather sluggishly from publisher to publisher—and my hand reflected them. Both Robert and I had, at various times, had our palms read and Yaria told neither of us anything particularly startling in addition to these previous readings.

But the cards were magnificent. This was at a time when Robert had not answered his father's offer, and when his father had assumed he was not interested, and when we both thought it would be impossible to leave Rome until December because of commitments we'd already made. The boat, the *Tana,* which I had never seen and which Robert had only slight acquaintance with, lay docked in New Jersey, and the winter weather had even then begun to limit its activity. We had come to Yaria because he was the only mystic source we had to immediately draw from, and because he knew nothing about either our plans or us. He brought out the cards and, placing the pack before him on the table, asked in his low voice if there was a question either of us would like to ask them. They would, he said, answer.

Historically, the Tarot cards are possibly the oldest symbolic records of mankind. There are theories of their origin which extend to nearly every corner of the world, but the most widely held of these place their beginnings in the East, probably in ancient Egypt at a time when it became necessary, for various reasons, to consolidate mystic knowledge into particular recorded forms. In addition to the fifty-six cards which have evolved into our modern-day playing cards, and which are likewise arranged in four suits, there are the more important and potent cards which make up what is called the Major Arcana. These twenty-two cards illustrate the various stages of progress and enlightenment through which the human soul passes, while at the same time corresponding to the separate meanings of the separate letters of the Hebrew alphabet. (They may, in addition, represent a period of history through this alphabet, and so be more than either alphabet or example; they may be the only existing record of pre-historical times, neatly done up, and thereby obscured, as both fable and function. But this is not yet a popular view.) Where and what these cards ultimately derive from has never, by any system of interpretation, been completely and factually explained; the most important fact of the cards is simply that they function, and this they do beautifully, without benefit of symbological etymology. They "work."

They work when an understanding of what their different faces represent is applied to answering questions of time, space, and particular probabilities. They work, and here their popularity lies, in the business of "telling fortunes."

Each of the seventy-eight cards has a particular meaning, the fifty-six cards of the Minor Arcana as well as those of the Major Arcana: meanings which have been passed down over centuries and which the "pictures" on the cards themselves, as clearly as they can, illustrate. A reader or witch such as Yaria depends upon these meanings to explain the particular answers to any given question, but also depends upon his own psychic intuition to make as specific as possible their more generalized images.

The four suits of the Minor Arcana each represent a different element of life. The Wands, which have changed in our present-day playing cards to the suit of Clubs, represent and partake of the element of Fire. Each of the meanings of the suit of Wands concerns itself to some degree with the growth of matter, with enterprise, with the beginnings and birth of all things, through Fire. The Cups, which have today come to be Hearts, partake of the element of Water. The fourteen cards of this suit all reflect in some way pleasure, through love, and through physical happiness. There is with Water a sense of pleasurable coming together, and at the same time, spirituality. The third suit, that of Swords, which is now Spades, has as its defining element Air, and as its basic character, strife. Air and Swords represent opposition and obstacles, complications in the way affairs are moving. The last element to be represented is Earth, and in the suit of Pentacles, now Diamonds, there is the definite smack of money attached to every card. The profitable manifestation of matter turns up in this suit, and the cards of Pentacles, in all the Tarot pack, are the ones most grounded in practicality. They signify the evident, the no-nonsense, and the quite unspiritual.

Depending on the position with regard to the other cards being laid out, and to the nature of the question asked, the meanings of these different elements and suits is determined. And the influence of the remaining twenty-two cards acts in combination with these suits to explain how such influences are, in relation always with the question, made manifest.

My question to the cards was, should I take a trip? I wanted to make the issue as simple as possible, so that the cards themselves could embellish it. They did. Yaria, reading in what seemed to be a variation of what I now know is the Tree of Life method, first said that the trip I was contemplating was not just an overnight junket, but was a serious undertaking that would last for a matter of months. He said I was interested in uncovering an ancient mysticism, something that involved a pre-Christian culture. He said that the search would be tied in with my work and would be a search by water, involving a large and a smaller body of water. And, he said, I would be accompanied by the man who was sitting next to me.

He went on to say that there would be a third person interested in making the trip with us, but that we should not allow anyone else to accompany us, also that there was danger of my being "incarcerated" in an area that was in the southwest corner of our itinerary. He said, finally, that the trip would be of great importance to both of us and would lead us into an interest in the occult that would be reflected in our work.

Robert's question was concerned with the outcome of his first novel, but the question of the trip kept coming through in his reading as well. We were going to team up, Yaria said, in some kind of joint enterprise after the trip was completed. And Robert was scheduled to do something in the way of journalism, or photography. Also there would be a second trip growing out of the first. He said we would not be able to start the actual journey until after the second week in November, because of obligations or complications. He said the trip would last six months. He said we would go.

He also replied, when I asked him if there was anything in the cards that indicated an earth change between that day and the time of our trip, that nothing would change. He seemed slightly puzzled by that question and dismissed it abruptly. The readings took less than an hour apiece; there were periods of silence between the various cards, and generally the atmosphere was soft and low-keyed. When we explained, after he had finished, what the trip was all about he seemed not at all surprised and only nodded politely. He told us as we left that we ought not to ask the cards anything more for three months, and then, matter-of-factly, he bid us good day.

Earlier I have mentioned the atmosphere in Rome as a factor in our beginning interest in Atlantis; as we gathered our resources more tightly together and became certain that we were indeed going to go off on the search, this atmosphere continued to serve our enthusiasm. For some reason, perhaps because of the rather ungainly weight of our twin egos, we not only accepted the fact that we were going, we as easily accepted the fact that we were going to find it, find some proof of Atlantis. A trip from Rome down to Corfu or Crete, being shorter in scope, might easily have given us less ambitious hopes; as it was, because of the colossal number of unknowns involved, we felt less hindered by scientific theories of improbability, and therefore less encumbered by a "realistic" attitude. In the full flush of total ignorance, we believed.

Yaria's reading of the cards reinforced the only kind of evidence we were allowing in our court of opinion—the psychic. Witches, dreams, and prophecy nudged us along so smoothly that, both then and now, I have never felt we had any choice but to follow their course and pursue their promptings. As we settled our affairs during those first weeks in October, gallery owners and bartenders tried to show us how mad we were, but in our slightly hysterical smugness we accepted no arguments other than in terms of the psychic facts themselves. We were beyond logic and were, of course, insufferable.

I fell off my horse for the last time at the Cinecitta stables and regretfully informed the casting director that I had been called back to the states for "personal reasons of conscience." The Greek actor, Cyrus Elias, with whom I'd been rehearsing laughed and swore at the ingratitude of canceled contracts and the incompetence of our corporate mind, but it was he who finally took us to the airport and admitted as we passed through the gate that he fully expected us to find . . . whatever it was we expected to find. We left on October 25, (the filming dates on the canceled contract extended through November 13) leaving behind a small circle of friends slightly dizzy with what had become their own as well as our chain of possibility and expectation.

In Wisconsin, where I flew for a few days to be with my family before joining Robert in New Jersey, the attitude of friends was decidedly different from that which it had been in Rome. There was a look of profound embarrassment in the faces of those few college friends I happened to run into, and my explanations of what I was doing these days became briefer and briefer. That attitude changed again when I spent any time in Manhattan, after a day of lessons on seamanship and charting with Robert's father: there was an immediate acceptance of the concept Atlantis, just as there was an interest in occultism in general, from those we met there. In fact, there seemed to be a bit too much. Whatever else the idea of the search had seemed in Rome, it hadn't seemed commonplace; what appeared once or twice in Manhattan was a spasm of interest that bordered on avant-gardism, that thought the idea of Atlantis terribly chic. Astrology ash tays were beginning to appear on coffee tables, and the instant familiarity that sun-sign labeling breeds at cocktail parties was gradually beginning to hold astrology up to contempt. Of the two extremes in attitude which I experienced in Milwaukee and New York, the former was easier to work with. Richard Ideman, the astrologer whom I'd exchanged dreams with from Rome, was pleased with the increasing number of subjects and students who were coming his way, but was slightly uneasy about the forms interest in astrology was taking. At the time, though, he seemed to think that, whatever led one to an interest in the occult or parapsychological, or to astrology, eventually the good would come through. (Last night, with a year elapsed and the search behind us, Robert, Richard, and I walked along the streets of the Upper East Side of Manhattan, where one bar was offering free drinks to Taurians and another was advertising the coming Saturday as Libra night. The good, we decided, was having a harder and harder time appearing.)

We spent, then, little time on the east side of the Hudson, sticking to our books and charts in New Jersey, only occasionally coming in to return books to Richard, who had become a source of even more works on Atlantis.

We maintained a curious balance. From the day we left Rome until the day we found ourselves alone with the *Tana,* we managed to hold our attitudes in a kind of pragmatic suspension. It was necessary for us to believe in the search we'd embarked on, along with our own function and relation to it, while at the same time believing that we were no more than the greenest novices in appreciating and understanding any psychic or occult phenomena. Still, there were traces of a sometimes giddy fatalism around the edges of our plans. We had begun to adopt an attitude—which we would later see working in our friend Margaret—of accepting the influences and experiences that occurred as being those necessary to our progress, and of not attempting to assimilate

51

too much that was out of our direct path. This served to reinforce our attitude of mission and also made the mission itself a good deal easier. As long as we felt we were being nudged toward something, we were willing to do everything we could to advance the progress, but if we ever felt that we ourselves were the prime movers, we stopped dead in our tracks. This happened seldom, only when one or the other of us stepped back from the experience and looked at our plans purely objectively through the bloodshot eyes of skepticism. Usually we were too busy to assume that stance, however, and so kept moving.

We had two names to make our progress down the Atlantic coast in this way easier. One was the man whose name had appeared in the article concerning the Atlantean "temple" off Andros, which I'd come upon in Rome, Dr. Manson Valentine. The other was a name Richard had supplied. A friend of his had attended a meeting of the New York branch of the Cayce Institute, or Association for Research and Enlightenment, at which a tape had been played concerning Atlantis exploration in the waters off the Bahama Islands. That name was Trigg Adams, and he invited anyone who was similarly interested to contact him at his Miami address. These names were the only contacts we had and, in the case of Dr. Valentine, there was neither address or number through which to trace him. But the names served. As long as there were two separate possibilities, as long as there were two people in the world more knowledgeable about Atlantis than ourselves, and as long as the names had been supplied to us, their importance to us was assured. They were important to us because balanced against the weight of Tarot cards and dreams, astrologers and witches, they were the closest things to facts that we had.

November was the month we pored over boating manuals and pamphlets on seamanship until the print swam, and practiced docking and embarking until the *Tana*'s gunnels nearly bled. It was a crash course, by any definition, but Robert's father, a member of the U. S. Power Squadron, somehow managed to prevail, and the *Tana* herself managed to survive. We were brilliant on adjusting the Loran radar lines and pinpointing our position while in dock; unfortunately we never had the desire or necessity to use that knowledge while under way.

Our other skills were less advanced, and conversely, were called upon in the course of the trip more frequently. It took me the space of four states before I could tie an efficient bowline, but I had the emergency call letters memorized the first day out. Robert was great on knots but not so good on colors. Like red and green.

But we learned enough, and quickly enough, so that by Thanksgiving both we and our instructor reluctantly admitted that we were ready to leave. The snow and freezing temperatures by then were beginning to slightly complicate our plans, and so we waited until the first, and then the second, and finally the third of December to pull away from the Bimini Yacht Club in Brielle, New Jersey, and to splash, numb and serene, into the waiting Atlantic.

II

Water

We would get up at first light, just as the whole half of the sky was beginning to pearl over. If the land was low along the horizon, or if we were close to the sea, you could tell what kind of air the day would bring from the small collection of clouds that rose with the sun. It was the time you felt healthiest, closest to the water, and happiest and most intelligent. And one deliberately thought how incomparably better this was than most everybody else's morning.

Up on the bridge we seldom talked for the first two hours of the day, except to ask if the other wanted more coffee, to point out a precocious bird, or to mention in the most perfunctory way that the next marker was to port or starboard.

You noticed something and stared at it, thinking of another, entirely different, thing. I liked to stare down at the wash pushed out from the bow. At fifteen knots, on smooth inland water, the tumble of foam was considerable and constant. And I would fantasize elaborately, while the water minded my eyes and kept them occupied, giving my mind freedom. When the sun had gone through its changes, from pink to bright lemon through vermilion and orange, and finally to an unassailable, rude, molten gold, and we felt its heat, we would begin to jabber, sometimes about the dawn's success, as if it had been a theatrical experience, or about what we had been thinking and what it meant to our respective and prospective novels. By ten, it was usually just another pretty day.

We left from Brielle, New Jersey, December 3, 1968, at seven in the morning, and moved out over water that was eerily calm and glassy, as smooth and neat as a matron's gray hair. We behaved a great deal like the principals in a cigarette commercial, drinking cup after cup of coffee and gazing with authority out over the horizon. We held to our compass course like Swedes, as if our lives depended on it, when actually the very familiar beaches of New Jersey were never more than a few hundred yards to starboard the whole time. But it was necessary, facing the unknown, to strike an attitude; and it was necessary, shouldering the responsibility of a thirty-thousand dollar boat, to pretend one was not completely alone: it was necessary, in short, to pretend this was a movie, that the situation was not real (which, anyway, it seemed not to be) and that behind us, and with the big rising sun on the extreme left of the screen, the credits moved at a more than readable pace. Such fantasies barely compensated for the fact that Michael and I had never been alone on the *Tana* before. One's father was not sitting close to the wheel, seemingly nonchalant, but ready to grab it at the first sign of danger. (He had taught me to drive the old

Buick in the same way—with his thumb on the wheel, as heavy, unobtrusive and effective as a butcher's.) Now we were alone and actually in charge of things, and if an engine stopped we would die and the boat would sink and one's father would be displeased. Imagining klieg lights and camera crews seemed to give us the confidence we needed to set sail that cold day in December. It was going to be a splendid movie.

It is comparatively easy now to look back, admittedly with a bit of nostalgic gloss, and account reasonably for the feelings we experienced in the face of a very loaded situation. We felt incredibly vulnerable. Six months later our astrologer friend, Richard Ideman, was to tell us that in reading our charts he had seen a great danger of both our deaths by water. He had considered wiring us (we were in Nassau at the time) but he figured wisely that we would still have to get the boat home and such a pronouncement would incapacitate us greatly. I am very pleased he didn't tell us. I have always vehemently hated the idea of death, perhaps unnaturally, and have studiously avoided the possibility of it happening to me. I mean I did not think of it much during the storms we encountered. I hated the idea of losing the boat, but thought we could both swim our way out of anything. I think probably there is a lot to be said for arguing down Death. To succeed one has to be aware of the possibility and then impertinently deny it. That sounds very foolish and trite, perhaps, and sooner or later I must be proven wrong. But why do certain people die so young, when others, who live comparably in much greater danger, survive to a great age? Maybe it's a question of personal philosophy. I believe it is a simple fact that all who habitually go

59

down to sea have a personal philosophy of life and death. They may not always be able to verbalize it, nor would they care to admit that they have or need one, but it is there, much more thoroughly developed than in the rest of us. One already is familiar with the superstitiousness of sailors, with the almost endless list of epigrams, legends, tales, remedies, and jargon which make the language of the sea an impossible thing to master unless you are born to it. More specifically, take the philosophy of feminization of all things nautical. Behind it, of course, is the effort to comprehend (or conquer) that which cannot be logically understood. But more than that, feminization is the philosophy by which all things, upon which one's life and safety depend, are given a personality—one that ranges from agreeable and co-operative to incredibly obstinate and deadly. A mizzen or an engine, it's all the same. If something goes wrong with one of them, there is spite, female spite involved. And if not, then there is love. A sailor's luck is merely the esteem in which he is held by his ship and her parts.

But like one's personal philosophy of life and death, this one is not always consistent with practical understanding or application. (The phenomenon of death exists and it can not be altered or avoided by definition.) However, exceptions to the rule can be explained quite simply. One can say, for instance, of a drowning sailor who cries, "But I loved her" as he goes down, that his intellectual approach to the sexual relationship between himself and his ship was for some reason abortive, and did not, when he needed it, stand him in very good stead with her. She betrayed him nonetheless, as women will do. For the sea, the greater, more powerful woman, is apt, in the face of an approach-avoidance, love-hate situation, to react more often as a slut than as a lady of quality.

That is, she will not always be willing to forgive him his mistakes; for in the lexicon of the sea, a mistake is an insult, and as we know, the majority of insulted women behave badly.

These generalities safely shot down, like so many skeets, if admittedly with the shotgun of inadvertency, we come to ourselves as sailors and the *Tana* as boat-woman. She is a fine boat for her size and type, a handcrafted, thirty-seven-foot Egg Harbor Sportfisherman Cruiser. She was built in 1966, and is equipped with Twin Chrysler Fury gasoline-burning engines, capable of developing 210 horsepower each. Her cruising range when we started was about two hundred miles, and in this fact lies the root of all our difficulties with her later on. She simply was not meant for long distance running. (For that you need diesels.) Her beam is thirteen feet, six inches, a very comfortable proportion for her length, and she is equipped with Loran as a navigational aid (which we never used) and of course a fathometer. She sleeps four comfortably, or six very good friends. She carries seventy gallons of water (good for one and a half showers), has a propane oven and range, an electric refrigerator and a good-sized freezer compartment. Her hull is wooden and her superstructure fiberglass and wood. The afterdeck and wheelhouse are teak, and her interior is paneled in African mahogany. She draws four feet. She cruises at 15 knots and has a top speed of 19 or 20. She was designed for the New Jersey waters, which is to say, she was designed for the Manasquan and Beach Haven inlets, famous for their huge following swells and unpredictability. She is at her best in a following sea, but she can go through anything for a short distance. What we wanted to do was take her through calm seas for a very long distance. So immediately she might have taken offense had she been brought up to do so.

But she had not. Before we left on this voyage, the *Tana* had never been more than a hundred miles or so from Brielle. She was used only for weekend fishing, or a pleasure jaunt in the bay. And I would think that even a livery horse, used to particular trails, would balk when, instead of turning back to the barn at a certain point, it was made to gallop further on across unproscribed stretches and over unfamiliar hedges.

But if she was not, as a woman, used to going very far from home, she was at least designed to be able to. She is, after all, a superb boat. But Michael and I were not born to be sailors. As of a month before leaving, Michael had never so much as been aboard a boat, apart from the usual rowboating in Central Park, and a short stint on a PT boat in a Bob Hope movie in Puerto Rico. I had been out fishing in the *Tana* four or five times, and once or twice I had taken the wheel for a few minutes, but I seriously did not know port from starboard until my father began teaching us in November.

And a month later we were alone at sea, pretending the situation was cinematic. You can understand, now, the necessity of such a pretense.

We brought with us fifty or sixty books, on Atlantis, archaeology, astrology, Cayce, history and legends, myths, plus novels and other entertainments. We had with us our typewriters and reams of paper, and Michael had brought his art materials. And on the way down we added to the library whenever we could, especially in Virginia Beach where we stopped to go to the Cayce Institute, the Association for Research and Enlightenment, more about which presently.

Our intentions, in the beginning, were so vague and our ideas on the subject of Atlantis so incomplete, that we took refuge in the possibility of research, in the possibility of defining the goals of our search before the time came to actually start achieving them. Michael was very definitely off to find the Lost Continent of Atlantis. He knew we would find it, just as surely as he knew it was there to find. I, on the other hand, believed in the idea of five or six months on a yacht in the Bahamas. Looking for Atlantis was an amusing cover, as far as I was concerned. Finding it was irrelevant to the real success of the voyage. I wished to start a new novel; I believed at the time that I might write a little something about the metaphor of Atlantis. This was a possibility, but I knew quite definitely that I would not have to find the place to be able to write a novel about it.

I had to be persuaded to leave Rome, for I had gotten myself to the point of loving the city more than any place in which I have ever lived. This, I know, is not a thoroughly original idea; it ranks, I suppose, with disliking New York, which I do, and I now anxiously anticipate leaving the second and returning to the first as soon as possible. I left primarily because I knew one could eventually return, and because we decided that the offer of the boat was too attractive to refuse.

The news that we were going was treated as bizarre and insane, not only in Rome, among our friends, as Michael has already described, but by members of my family. Certain of them insisted my father call the whole thing off, on the grounds that he had not thought the thing through, and had not any real idea of the dangers involved. But in the course of negotiations I had made him promise that once we had decided, nothing, from ice floes to bankruptcy, could keep us from going. Ten days later we left Rome and began a month's instructions, and all too soon we found ourselves at the point to which I have brought you, a half mile off the Jersey coast, and fifty miles or so into our search for Atlantis, a search that would cover nearly four thousand miles.

One's idea of how it was going to be at sea in December was pretty much borne out. A bit colder perhaps, but as pretty and gray as you would imagine; and exhilarating and frightening and exciting. We had picked our departure day well. You seldom see the ocean as flat and docile, as if it were this way solely to please and reassure us. It turned out, in fact, to be an ambush.

At one o'clock in the afternoon we pulled into a marina in Cape May, at the tip of New Jersey. It was a very stupid thing to do considering the early hour and flat seas—anyone else would have been able to read the signs and make time. But, immensely pleased with ourselves for the way this first day had gone, we stopped there. And for the next two days, we sat out fifty-mile-an-hour winds, sleet, rain, and snow, and had the feeling that after all the hoopla of preparing for a great long trip, we were never going to get out of our own back-yard.

The following day even the water in the sheltered marina was choppy and bitter. Out checking our lines for the tenth time, we met and began talking with a married couple whose boat, the *Gladius X,* was docked nearby. I had been looking forward to the reactions of people to why we were making this trip. But Lynn and Val Murphy, our new friends, seemed not in the least intrigued that we were writers on our way to find the lost continent. It's not that they weren't surprised by what we told them. I think they were; but they made every effort to studiously ignore it. It was as if we had said several people we knew had died and we were going to collect their bodies—as if it were not polite to talk about it. Perhaps, being still so far north, where the idea of Atlantis is generally considered to be extravagant, we were not taken seriously.

That evening the four of us went out to the beach for a closer look at the weather. The night was dark but moony, and the water was terrifically rough. The waves seemed unreasonable, making as much for the open sea as for land. Michael noticed something about a quarter of a mile out and Val said, Oh, that's the U.S.S. *Atlantis*. She said it cheerily, with a bright note in her voice, as if to say this was as far as any Atlantis legend should properly be allowed to go. It had been one of three experimental concrete ships, made by the British during World War I. The experiment had not worked out and after three crossings the *Atlantis* was bought by the U. S. Coast Guard to be used as a pier. But even that plan could not be managed because she broke in half, in a storm much like the one we were watching. Understandably, Michael and I were transfixed by this piece of news. The Murphys rattled on about other things, and because no verbal connection between the ship and our trip had been made, we both felt it very important to assimilate as much of the occasion's significance as we could. The U.S.S. *Atlantis*. We asked Val what had happened to the other two ships. She didn't know. But later on we were to find another of them, this time off South Bimini. And it was as if two gigantic cookie-crumb clues had been left for Hansel and Gretel on their way through the enchanted forest.

The next morning, December 6, we decided to make for Ocean City, Maryland, accompanied by the *Gladius X*. Winds were fifteen to twenty, with gusts up to thirty, and our course would bring us across the mouth of the Delaware Bay and River. Promised were wicked seas, not especially high, but very sharp and insidious.

We took off five minutes before the *Gladius X,* which had to take on fuel. We came out of the inlet looking all about and thinking that it all didn't seem too bad. But as we turned, just out of the inlet, to assume our compass course, a high random wave came up over the bridge and caught us both full in the face. The aim was dead-on and we were drenched and immediately freezing cold. (We had not even had the sense to put on foul-weather gear.)

We turned back. I was furious and said a good many dirty words. Still the *Gladius X* had not appeared in the inlet. Michael said nothing, being too cold to talk. Then we decided to turn again, and make the trip after all. I think it was because I was so angry; thinking that one couldn't very well be angry with the sea, I became angry with my own stupidity and ineptness as a pilot. It was obvious we hadn't learned a thing on the calm seas of the first day. Today would have to be different. We would make it or drown, or we would go back home for lack of fun.

The *Gladius X* soon came out of the inlet and throttled up to what we thought was a very stagy 22 knots. It flew by us, the Murphys waving cavalierly from the bridge, all bundled up and dry in bright red rubber overalls and hoods. Perhaps they didn't remember our top cruising speed was 16 knots. They were also, somehow, on a somewhat different heading. (Lynn, seeing how bad the water was, had very wisely decided to make a bit for the open and calmer seas.) We were perfectly terrified at being left behind. We throttled up to about 18 knots for a while to close the gap, but it was useless trying to catch them. After a few minutes, during

66

which we were repeatedly drenched, we slowed down to 16 again, a speed which was better for the *Tana* but very bad for taking on wash. There was nothing to do but shiver and steer.

Ahead of us, the *Gladius X* became smaller and smaller. Then she must have slowed down a bit because, about two miles off, her size remained constant. She was not going to leave us.

Next, we went about taking steps to make ourselves more comfortable. Michael went down and changed and put on foul-weather gear. Then he took the wheel down in the wheelhouse, and I changed. As we did this, the seas got progressively rougher.

An hour or so out, we caught up with the *Gladius X.* Stopped and pitching wildly, her port engine had failed. So at about 5 knots, we both crossed the mouth of the Delaware. Because of the wash, visibility was terrible. In the wheel-house, fishing rods, gear, books, charts, chairs, everything, was tossed back and forth, up and down. Nothing broke, but everything moved. It was as if we were in the vortex of a poltergeist. Our arms ached from holding on. And every few seconds a big wave would catch us and the boat would make hideous sounds, wood and glass sounds, like crates of beer being dropped on cement from a height. We tried to raise the *Gladius X* on our radio, but being only a few yards from us, its radio beam was amplified to the point of unintelligibility. Val sounded like Donald Duck in a rage. (All we had had to do was switch off the aerial, but who knew?)

Lynn, meanwhile, was out in his cockpit, crawling around his wounded engine. I wondered if we would have to tow her, and pictured the *Tana*'s gunnels being ripped out by the line. But finally we made it into the lee of Maryland and the water was simplified into a strong following sea. And then, about the same time, the *Gladius X*'s port engine was revitalized, and we both took off, to make a glorious, swift and smooth entrance into the Ocean City inlet, and thence to Capt. Wm. Bunting's marina, at three-thirty in the afternoon. Below, nearly every shelf in the cabin had been emptied into the center of the floor.

While we were washing down the boats, the Murphys thanked us for having stayed with them when their engine failed. And I wondered if, had the situation been reversed, they would have thought they had a choice.

After dinner, the winds dropped and shifted. Outside, the sea was a grainy mirror beneath a full moon, and Lynn advised a midnight creep to Portsmouth. We declined, being very tired, still scared and in no particular rush. The next morning the *Gladius X* was gone.

I remember that the next morning was brisk, but nicer than the day before. Again the seas were following, yet in a different way. At fifteen knots we moved just behind the swells, but every now and then one would catch us and we would have a kind of surfboard ride that lasted a minute or two. Then the bow would dip over the crest and down into the trough and we would take on some wash and slow down. It was a pitchpolling situation and the first time it happened, I was terrified. A boat pitchpolls when her bow gets buried in the back side of the wave in front, and a following wave lifts her stern at the same time, making her tumble end over end. But of course that didn't happen. The seas weren't quite high enough and the swells too far apart.

We moved down the coast of Maryland, and then of Virginia. By early afternoon, the water had begun to pick up a bit, not badly, but enough to indicate a trend, and we decided to put into the Wachapreague Inlet for the night. We were now one day out of the Chesapeake Bay, which, we had been told, would either make or break us, and we must approach it with care and only in good weather.

But the Wachapreague Inlet is not considered a likely stopover for boats going north or south. It is very shallow, badly marked, and leads not to a bay but to an almost endless system of marshland channels. It took us forty-five minutes to get to Wachapreague proper, a tiny town, with one marina, closed for the winter. We docked anyway, and immediately it began to snow. A group of small boys and dogs watched us tie up. The dockmaster they said, was off duck hunting. We had dinner aboard, and, with the heaters on, it was very warm and comfortable below. The snow became icy and rattled on the decks. Then when a blanket of it had been laid down, the sound ceased and it was very still. We went out on the dock. There were other boats but they were all dark, and none of them was as big as the *Tana*. We stood up on the dock and watched her for a while, talking about her, about how well she had done so far. We started to board her again, Michael had already jumped onto the gunnel, when there was a large blue and white electrical spark beside me where the boat's umbilical cord was plugged into the dock. All but the ship's battery lights had gone out. Including the heaters.

After an hour or so of our fiddling with the cord and plug, the dockmaster's son appeared, and he and another man with a big dog named Major came aboard to carve up and rearrange the shorted wires. But this time the plug blew out the entire dock. The dockmaster's son gave us an

Aladdin kerosene lamp heater for the night. Soft, feathery snow continued to fall. On the radio we picked up WAVA in Wheeling, got news of more bad weather and listened to "He's in the Jailhouse Now" and "Walkin' the Dog." It was very cold. Had the water been fresh, we would have been frozen in by morning.

When we woke up the boat was sheeted in ice. But the sun shone with an incredible brightness and the air was so fresh you wanted to shout into it. We were two more days stopped there with snow on our white decks. In the afternoon a black dog barked at us, and the children stood about at low tide watching. Then the third morning sun melted the snow and dropped the wind. A dark old man who shoveled clams from the bottom of a muddy skiff looked up as we dropped our lines and said, "That's a right smart lady." And we took in our lines and slid off through the low marshes back out to sea.

It was Tuesday, December 10, and in spite of a forecast of developing high northwest winds, we moved down the Virginia coast toward Chesapeake Bay. We knew it would be bad in the bay, but the radio had predicted more snow and rain, and higher winds for tomorrow. So it had to be that day.

Throughout the early morning the water was rough and high but following—the kind of sea which teaches you to pilot. We roller-coasted along about two miles offshore. Lynn Murphy had warned us about a set of shoals in the thirty-foot water, so we moved out a bit to go around them. But at the same time fog began to set in and as a result we missed the admittedly wide entrance to the bay. When we picked up the next buoy and realized our mistake, we were already southeast of the bay. And so we were forced to turn about and head directly northwest. What had been a swift, but practically comfortable, following sea was now a vicious head sea.

It was very cold and the wheelhouse windshield was icing. Visibility was only as far ahead as the next gigantic swell, and probably our greatest danger was collision, though at the time there seemed more immediate dangers.

The water got progressively worse as we headed into the bay, and the house and bridge were constantly awash. The buffeting was terrific. Designed not to pound or slap, she did both, until the starboard V bunk, forward, was ripped right out of the wall. And then at the worst of it, Michael began a necessarily clumsy but exceedingly manic soft-shoe routine; that is, he began to reject the whole situation as improbable, which proved its ludicrous self-evidence, which caused him to improvise on the humor of it. It was the same as that last scene in *Dr. Strangelove* when the jet bomber pilot drops out of the plane, riding the hydrogen bomb like a cowboy.

Once we passed over the tunnel-bridge things calmed down; without the constant wash the windshield began to earnestly freeze over, so we were forced to go back up to the bridge. For the next hour we were as cold and unhappy as I have ever been. One was tempted to cry, but tears on one's cheeks would have finished one off in that temperature. So moans sufficed. Time passed and we made it into the inner bay and the Elizabeth River, and then to the Holiday Harbor Marina, where out of a basic need to verbalize the experience, we complained to the dockmaster. He laughed at first, but later I overheard him describing us to someone as "two guys as mean as snakes."

It had been prearranged with my father that I call him

71

before and after the Chesapeake run, to make sure we had made it. I had called him two days before, from Wachapreague, but not since, and because he had not subsequently heard from us, he had begun to worry. Since no one had been at the Wachapreague Marina to answer its phone, he had been forced to call the sheriff of a neighboring town, who on Tuesday morning drove thirty miles to Wachapreague to see if we had left. We had. My father then called out the Coast Guard from Ocean City, Maryland, to Norfolk. By the time we had refueled, docked, thawed out, and pulled ourselves together enough to call him, he had presumed us dead. He knew about the weather, and he said we were crazy to have tried it. But he was pleased to feel that if we had weathered this we could get through just about anything. I said we had used up all our water in Wachapreague, had no heat or electricity and there had been another big storm coming. He said, Well, good. . . . Is the boat all right? I said yes, we were looking forward to being on the inland waterway from now on. He said, yes, so was he.

Getting to Portsmouth had been a full-time job, so much so that except for the books we were reading when we docked along the way, we seldom if ever thought or talked about Atlantis. I had developed an almost painful sense of responsibility for the *Tana*. I wanted things to go well, and survival meant paying attention to what we were doing. But now we had arrived and stopped for the time being. The boat was fine, safely moored, and the Edgar Cayce Institute, the Association for Research and Enlightenment, was just twenty miles away in Virginia Beach.

The next morning, a bus carried us there. The house looks like an unfinished Victorian resort hotel, except that

[1] Evangelo, the Bahamian fisherman who led the expedition to the find. *(Photo by Renee Turolla.)*

[2] The *Tana,* on the Inland Waterway.

[3] Divers, Count Turolla and Carter Lord, provide a point of reference for the size of the 'sea-wall' rocks.

[4] Note the many right angles and the way the stones are fitted together into a pattern. The large stone in the bottom of the photograph is approximately twelve feet across.

[5] This is one of the sections still slightly obscured by marine growth, encrustations and sand, plus, in the foreground, a school of fast moving fish. But even here, the pavement effect is evident.

[6] The rocks on the right are approximately five feet across, two feet thick, and very nearly square. The rectangular stones, when they occur, all lie in an east-west direction.

[7] Carter Lord, who is 6 ft. 2 in., diving close to some of the smaller stones.

[8] Evangelo, the Bahamian guide, informed us that the majority of the stones were covered over periods of two to three years by tidal sands. Here is a section being gradually uncovered. Largest stone, center right, is about eight feet long.

Victorian houses usually are higher than they are broad, and this was, if anything, squat-looking. It seemed stripped, as if all the gingerbread had been removed. In its way it is imposing but not because of any architectural importance.

It is better I think that Michael's journal tell you about the place. His opinion of it is more complete, since he stayed there for a weekend while I went to Washington. He appreciates it more and for different reasons, because he arrived believing in all of it—Cayce, the Institute, Atlantis—whereas I did not. I am still not sure about a lot of it. I work it out as I go along. I feel sorry for that man Plato. Half the world misunderstands him, and no one knows which half.

Friday, December 13, 1968, Michael's Bimini Journal:

We expected the Cayce Institute, or as it is called, the Association for Research and Enlightenment, to be some sort of monument to spook kitsch. It is, however, rather understated than gaudy, and the tone is, overall, one of muted accents and quiet energy. Tonight, after a long and solitary walk along the beach, I do feel that whatever emanations the building itself gives off are positive and benign. The Institute sits high on a hill which slopes down to the highway and then the sea, behind it is a wild, slightly overgrown area of marsh and pine. Floors creak and doors gently knock at night, but there is no hint of anything malevolent in the air. Just a great deal of slightly unsettling energy.

Yesterday Robert and I arrived by bus from Norfolk, on the way making the acquaintance of a young girl from just outside London who'd come over to work at the Institute. She was warm and informative and eager to tell us about the growing interest of young people in Cayce and in the Institute itself. The ARE was founded as an open-member-ship research society, in 1932, with its aim the further investigation of Cayce's readings, as well as other related psychic phenomena. Since then the building that now houses it has gone through a few changes, sheltering alternately WACs and Shriners, but restoring itself to the Institute as its headquarters in 1954. When we arrived, we introduced ourselves to Adelaide Crockett, the lady in charge of the library, and immediately she began pulling whatever books she thought pertinent off the shelves. Through the afternoon and evening we browsed and made notes and slowly realized that the bulk of Atlantology was no more factual or enlightening than our own dreams. Some of the various authors' books are fascinating, some just a procession of rococo fantasies, and some, surprisingly, tracts of insidious racism. The actual life-readings which Cayce gave are exceedingly difficult to absorb because of their syntax, but the more one reads of them the easier to understand they become. (Which is not to say that they are ever completely comprehensible, any more than vintage Stein or Joyce or Zarathustra.) One sentence emerges, however, that needs no qualification or interpretation; "Poseidia will be among the first portions of Atlantis to rise again—expect it '68 or '69—not so far away," from a reading made in June 1940. This is the statement that in various forms is making the psychic rounds, and the one that has engendered this year's activity of exploration. And this is the statement that, still and yet, I believe.

In Virginia Beach there are, it appears, a variety of ways to believe. Some of the ladies and gentlemen sitting about in chairs, and some of the teen-agers who charge in and out through the screen doors, are grounded in a rather fundamental Christian approach to mysticism and the occult. And an equal number probably take Christianity only as an interesting manifestation of psychic power. Jesus Christ

74

emerges variously as the one true Savior of the world, as a master of occult mysteries, or as simply a very beautiful man. (There is a horror which ARE members feel about the possibility of the emergence of a Cayce "cult." They feel, and with good reason, that any real enlightenment the readings have to offer can very easily be swamped in an excess of shiny-eyed zeal and Bible-belt fervor. One is welcomed to the Institute whether he be verifiably sane or not, but he is not made privy to the body of the organization until he has demonstrated a certain degree of religious, or mystical, realism and common sense.)

It is after midnight, however, and common sense seems, for a while to have passed me by. It has been, all in all, a thoroughly strange day; Robert left for Washington early this morning, and I have spent the day in the library and on the beach and in the company of a woman who appeared out of the rain in a parrot-pink hat late this afternoon. (In the library, talking to the librarian between books, she suggests I phone a woman who is interested in Atlantis and who has a home here in Virginia Beach. She says the woman's name is Mrs. Adams. Before I can follow up and telephone her, this short Englishwoman bustles into the library, slightly damp around the edges, but—and it is perhaps because of the pink hat—sparkling.) After a few moments, the two of us are introduced by the librarian and retire to the foyer for some serious chatter. Her name is Marguerite Barbrook and she has come over from her home in Mallorca, is staying at the home of Mrs. Adams—who, it turns out, is the mother of Trigg Adams—and has been for some time roving secretary to Egerton Syke's Atlantis Research Society.

When I tell her about our trip, the boat, and our itinerary, her enthusiasm and interest progresses from sparkling to nearly blinding and she immediately begins writing out names and addresses which I am to call and write to in

75

Miami Beach. The Adams name is scored and underscored, and it seems increasingly inevitable that we will be in some kind of contact. We adjourn, the two of us, to the Adams house for coffee. Mrs. Adams has gone to her Miami Beach house for the holidays, and Mrs. Barbrook is considering alternately about fifteen trips she herself plans to make. There is a possibility that she will be coming down to Florida after the first of the year for a bit. She is charming and witty, and of course I will call whatever numbers and names she gives me, and gladly. (As it turns out, her address book has been misplaced, and when I leave her it is with one or two more names but' no more numbers than I've had in New York. But, as she says, no matter.) We talk for two or three hours about Rome and England, the occult, Cayce, writing, and various methods of prophecy—all subjects turning on the pivot of Atlantis, and I leave looking forward to the possibility of seeing her in January or February. I am sorry that Robert has missed her.

Tomorrow maybe a few more books and articles and then a noon bus back to Norfolk and Portsmouth.

The opinion I had of myself was particularly high that weekend in Washington. It was good to be off the boat for a while, good to be staying in a hotel, something I have always loved, good to have brought along with me, like an extra costume, the desire and patience, introspection and pride of one who talks regularly with the famous dead. Standing in the rain in Arlington Cemetery, I was able to think as I had certain mornings on the *Tana,* when the day was just beginning and you could still look directly into the sun. I might be living out the thoughts of a few days before. And now, today, I think that having gone to Washington makes it no more real in my mind as a memory than my having conjured up a conversation with Paul of Tarsus. And it seems that had I had the time and opportunity, I might have actually given life to a great many people and places, taken side trips all over the world—except that by the time you have realized the secret and significance of something like this, it is long gone and out of reach.

When I got back to Portsmouth and went aboard the *Tana* again, it was as if I were stepping into a taxicab which had brought me someplace, had waited for me at the curb, and was now prepared to take me anywhere I wished to go.

We spent the next eight days on the Intracoastal Waterway. This part of the trip was more as I had imagined it would be, through canals, rivers, bays, sounds—all calm waters and well marked. After a week of empty seascapes and deserted winter beaches, we were dazzled by the scenery. That first day, December 16, we went by the Norfolk Fleet at anchor and in mothballs, and you thought they must be working it all out with mirrors because it was difficult to believe so many ships could be positioned in such a long row so perfectly. And there were barges and bridges and scores of factories and particularly American arrangements of stacks and smoke; and moving trains and spidery trestles and winter trees that looked burned out. Black catfishermen waved. And later we passed backyards, thick woods, unclaimed fields, open marshes, small towns where only fishermen and a few farmers lived. We went through the Virginia Cut to Coinjock, where the next day we had our first inland morning and a dawn so still we might have been woven into a tapestry. It was pink and cold, and dark green in the belly of the trees across the canal. I am a child from the city, sent to see such things for myself.

Sixty miles to Belhaven across the Albemarle Sound, duck soup after the Chesapeake; we blast across it through a light rain, the water pine-needle-brown and choppy, the air wet, fast, and gray. We overtake a Canadian flautist, whom we have met in Portsmouth, in his sailboat, recognizable by its mastlessness, and breezily pass by.

The ice has caught up to us the next morning in Belhaven. It is still dark. Just beyond the pilings of the dock we feel rather than see the sliver ice. It is like a sugar glaze on the water. We inch back to the dock for a council with the crew of another boat, the *Wilco*, same size as the *Tana*, but with a fiberglass hull that can take the ice. We move slowly out of Belhaven together, and the water is thick and heavy, like maple syrup or velvet. I have never seen water like that. There is no ice, but we keep going slowly because any second we may hit a patch of it. The *Tana* is just a length behind the *Wilco*, in the port half of her wake. But both our wakes are foamless, unbroken, and indolent. They are two long inverted V's that fan from our sterns in a lovely, soft geometry, and the two boats and two V's move along, all bound up together so that nothing moves and all of it does, like one ship past a mirror. We stay with the *Wilco* for three days, down to St. Simon's Mills, Georgia.

In the mornings we start off before dawn, following the *Wilco*'s lights, which wink out now and then like fireflies. After an hour one of us makes breakfast, which we eat on the flying bridge. The light has brought porpoises in pairs, sliding like chunks of putty and chrome in and out of the water. We watch for logs and birds.

There are shipbuilders on ladders, hammering and sanding

skeletal hulls. Two groups, one black and one white, stand on the starboard bank of a river, watching a man in a rowboat grapple for a missing person. At last Spanish moss appears, on both banks, in South Carolina. A man waves to us from the yard of his house, next to an American flag on a very high pole. We run 160 to 180 miles a day, from before dawn to after sunset; long, exhausting, beautiful days that grew warmer.

Michael's *Bimini Journal* records virtually everything that happened to us. It contains, probably, thousands of facts, like a memory bank: what we ate for breakfast, what books we read, who we met, what they were wearing, their pets' names; everything. I could make chronological entries for the rest of the trip to Miami Beach that would stun you with detail.

But I have tried that, been bored with it, and have realized that no amount of detail can suggest the significance of any occurrence, or make up for the lack of it. And it is lack of significance, or of central unifying ideas, that make journals, generally, a waste of time. All the journals I have ever seen have had the total indiscrimination of daily life. They see everything as potentially important, valuable, worth saving, worth writing down. For a serious writer, this can be insidious. All things, all events, all pretty sunsets and dramatic dawns, are *not* important, are *not* symbolic, and will not make a difference in his life as an artist. But a Journalist, or Diarist will, in his mad eclecticism, think they might, and rush to write them down.

The result is generally a bore. It may serve to help the writer recall an incident in detail, but I think that in writing the thing down in the first place, he has altered it somehow, altered what he might have remembered naturally; and when, years later, he goes back to the experience in his journal, he discovers fact, the moment's bias and art have become confused, and the significance of the event is hopelessly out of focus, if not completely lost.

I have read somewhere that all of a baby's future, each incident in his life, every word he'll ever speak, his entire life and his death, are in his first ass-slapped cry for breath. And one day, we will be able to decode those cries. A baby's first statement will be his complete autobiography. But that short cry will be the reduction of everything to pure significance. That is what I think a book should try to do. I cannot, therefore, pretend that the stops one makes on the way to a desert island are more important than one's desire, one's need, to escape to it in the first place. It is edited memory that keeps us sane and makes art. Happiness and beauty are almost always retrospective.

We arrived in Miami Beach two days before Christmas, and were surprised only by the fact that, never having been there before, we knew the city so well. Nothing that has ever been said about Miami Beach is exaggerated. Its counterpart, however, Miami, is quite another thing. It is the most Cuban, least American, city in the United States. One has the feeling of having crossed a border to get there. Small plaques in store windows read, "English spoken." And one knows with certainty that somewhere, in a nightclub, in a brothel, at a private party, somewhere, a slow dark lady is entertaining the boisterous crowd with a donkey. It is easy to conclude, even from the taxicab, that Miami Beach is dead and Miami is alive and sweating.

Christmas Day was warm and quiet. We had hangovers from Christmas Eve and got up late in the afternoon. We sat in the stern as the sun went down, still with headaches but feeling well enough, talking about what we would do for the evening, it being, after all, Christmas. We mentioned Margaret Adams and her son, Trigg, and Manson Valentine —three names that held equal importance to us, peopleless names. We borrowed a corkscrew from the 130-foot yacht *Lauvonnia* and had glasses of wine. It was getting dark. We wondered why Mrs. Adams had not returned either our letter from Virginia Beach, our three phone calls, or our message tacked onto her apartment door on Hibiscus Island, across the bay. Two friends we had met the night before called to ask us to a Jai Alai match in Miami. We declined, saying we were meeting a lady.

We had dinner aboard and just afterward the dockmaster returned to say there was another call for us, a lady named Mrs. Adams.

Margaret Adams is a woman of means who has been married and divorced four times, but it seems to me that these two facts do not go very far in describing her. She drives a Rolls-Royce that she has had painted pink. She is somewhere in her fifties, I suppose. She has white hair that was once red, and very fair skin. I have never seen her in anything but pink or tan.

Margaret is not one's Auntie Mame. Such people don't really exist, but the analogy helps in beginning a description of her. She is wonderfully strong, canny, and transparent. She has been married four times because she "marries" herself to all her interests. She involves herself completely in things and lacks the frivolity one needs to have an idea and not follow it through. She believes in impulses. One knows she is not where she is supposed to be at any given time, because one knows that by then she will have had an idea and gone off to pursue it. In this she is very nearly a fatalist. She drifts with what she is certain is a major tide, and she trusts life's instincts. If, for example. she is late for an appointment, or is forced to miss it completely, her excuse later on will be amazingly worthwhile. Her wrong turns are invariably proven right. Her sense of inadvertency is perfect. She could have been, if her spirit had not led her elsewhere, that quiet lady in the small, peculiar house at the end of the street, who thanked you for mowing her lawn every Wednesday afternoon, or who bought magazines from you twice a year.

Margaret stood on the dock and called to us. She was wearing a big pink cape, pink slacks, and she carried a tan canvas or leather pocketbook, the size of a shopping bag. We helped her aboard because the low tide made it an awkward step down to the gunnel.

"She's beautiful!" Margaret said. "What's her name?"

"The *Tana*."

"The *Tania?*"

"*Tana.*"

But it was too late. Margaret still mispronounces the name. But it doesn't matter; ultimately, they both mean gypsy.

We went below and sat around the table in the galley. We had some of the wine from dinner. For a while it was difficult to start. I believe Margaret's purpose in coming over was to see if we were serious about looking for Atlantis, plus, of course, she was interested in meeting new people. She asked us first how we had gotten interested in the project, and we told her about Rome and Yaria, the fortune-teller. We told her we wished to write novels about Atlantis, for that was our purpose then.

It was a good way to get started, but really, all we needed

was an excuse, a primer. In five or ten minutes we were rapping enthusiastically. I think Margaret and I sensed a strong affinity to each other immediately. Toward the end of the evening she suggested that she and I had probably had familial relationships with each other in past lives. There have been times since that first evening, when I have found it necessary to give her a very fatherly bit of advice, which usually she has accepted as gospel, and times when I find myself performing in front of her like a small child just home from school.

After a short while she started pulling photographs out of her pocketbook. With these pictures she introduced the cast of characters we would be involved with later on: Her son, Trigg, who was a commercial airline pilot; Dr. Valentine, Marguerite Barbrook, whom Michael had met in Virginia Beach, and a few others.

She was very honest about not being able to tell us too much now. She represented, she said, the Marine Archaeology Research Society (M.A.R.S.), which she and her son had formed for the expressed purpose of finding and researching Atlantis in the Bahamas. It was a non-profit corporation, and they were very anxious to make sure that people's motives were where they should be before being made privy to the society's information. But by the end of the evening she said she was convinced we had been sent from Rome to help in the search. The idea was very flattering and we felt a bit like aquatic messiahs.

She brought out some charts. She drew us a picture of the Andros "temple." She said she had some obviously man-carved rocks from the "temple's" foundation in the trunk of her car, that they smelled terribly, and that we would see them later that evening when she said good night.

83

Then we began to talk about other things not directly connected with M.A.R.S. She told us wonderful stories about regressions and psychometrizing, precognitive dreams, Edgar Cayce and the Institute, her affinity for the color pink, and I began to realize that while she talked of things for which, three hundred years ago, she could have been burned, she managed to sound perfectly unstrung and really rather logical. At the last minute she would practically step back from what she was saying and suggest that perhaps it was all nonsense and we should approach it cautiously. Or she would finish an anecdote with a dream which had led her to a peculiar lady with the unreasonable belief that cats could suck the life from a sleeping baby at night, and wasn't that preposterous. There was, in other words, a thin line beyond which one did not care to go. Tell me your dreams. Describe our past lives together; think of the goodness and love that one spirit can impart to another, living or dead. But, please, none of that talk about men in dark suits, or space ships disappearing around the dark side of the moon. It became immediately obvious that Margaret was in this for the good she could do with it, for what she could learn, for what she could give to others, and to give herself something to do that was useful, would amuse her, and was anything but a waste of time.

We had rather obliviously floated down the Waterway thinking that when we got to Miami we would try to make some contact, or find information that would send us off in some particular Atlantean direction. We were, at the most, hopeful of finding something that would keep us busy while we were not writing our novels, though we were, at the least, prepared for the possibility that we would continue to float about, getting tan, finding nothing in particular and having a good, lazy time. So to meet Margaret and to tie into what was actually a serious attempt to find Atlantis, made us think that perhaps we *had* been sent from Rome. It was Margaret who was not too bashful to say that since we were all investigating a Cayce prediction (namely that Atlantis would show definite signs of having existed, around Bimini, in 1968–69) it was not too unrealistic to believe that Cayce himself was the real organizer of the expedition, and the one to determine who should be included in it. This to me is an extravagant idea. But believing in it harmed no one; it only pointed to the fact that Margaret has met many ghosts in her life and I have as yet met none.

The expedition was planned for the first or second week in February, which was more than a month away. There would be plenty of time to make arrangements, fix dates and meeting places. Margaret said she would be in touch with us. We gave her two future addresses, one in Nassau, and one on Bimini that we thought would be likely stops for us. She said not to worry, she would find us. We gave her the boat's radio call numbers. She would either wire or phone or write us. But the concept to grasp, she said, was that what was to come off would come off, and worrying would not change it.

Perhaps I felt a pang of guilt, in the face of all this trust and openness, for I confessed then that I did not have Michael's or her faith in the occult, mysticism, ESP, etc.; was struggling, in all candor, to maintain an open mind about whether Atlantis had ever really existed or not; had never had any psychic experiences, never even remembered my dreams, and was not even convinced of the validity of anything Edgar Cayce had ever said. And Margaret said very kindly that this was certainly nothing to apologize about, and anyway, it seemed to her that I was as psychic as hell. And also, she said, looking about her, here was the *"Tania,"* just when she was needed, and two young people who could handle boats beautifully. We beamed. She told us to have a good time, collected all her photos, charts, pink pens and notes, kissed us good-by, and sped off in her rock-laden car.

We stayed in Miami Beach until two days after the New Year. Again, in reading it over, I find Michael's journal very close to fascinating, but even spiders are fascinated by themselves. And I wonder if such detail as filled our days is of any real importance at all. I would say we worked on the boat, which had become very dirty, spent time at various beaches, where the unattractives sat about like dollops of cottage cheese, and went to movies or bars at night. The journal sets it down as standard diaristic fodder, neither judging nor embellishing. I would transpose it into microcosmic Americana. Probably it could be easily done.

It was during this period, our first inactivity after two weeks of long-haul running, that I awoke at about four each morning, demanding to know where we were and what was happening. It would seem to me that both of us should not be sleeping at the same time, and I would rush up to the wheelhouse to grab and turn the wheel away from the dock. I did this five mornings in a row, once almost slicing a toe off on a chrome fitting. Meanwhile, Michael would be dreaming fitfully of Atlantis, of cataclysms, of burned faces, of tidal waves, and he would wake up thinking his dreams were coming true. It was a bad way to start the day. On the fifth morning Michael, being in between dreams at the moment, told me to shut up and go back to bed, and the next day I slept through until nine.

Two men, one of whom was named Rabbit, spent four days restaining and varnishing the double stern doors, which

86

had begun to peel from the constant salt bath of the trip. I got new straps made for the Bimini suntop. We scrubbed the teak, which had gotten very gray, and the brightwork, and cleaned the windows and ports. We even got out the dinghy and cleaned the hull with soap and water. The engines were checked and they seemed to be doing well, though one of the starboard tachometer batteries had to be replaced. We had the propane gas tanks filled, bought the necessary Bahama charts, a yellow quarantine flag for entering a foreign port, and got a replacement for the hauser cap we had lost in the Chesapeake. It was a week of lists and busy work.

Docked nearby was a sixty-five-foot yacht about twenty years old which looked brand new. I asked the dockmaster about her, and he said she was owned by a very old couple who seldom took her out. Her captain and mate lived aboard, and were famous for the anal-retentive attitude they took toward their charge. Everything glistened. The entire boat was gone over every morning. They worked on her constantly, shining this, painting that. There was, reputedly, not a nick, not a scratch, not a speck of dirt anywhere. I used to watch the mate every morning as he went through the cleaning routine. The *Tana* was much smaller, of course, but many of the jobs were similar, so I would clean along with him. It was better than making out lists of things that had to be done. After a few days of this, the captain of the other boat looked across and said to me, "Nice boat." I was very pleased and knew we could take off for Bimini any time now.

The last day of 1968 was warm and placid. Rabbit and his partner put the fourth and last coat of varnish on the doors. They would be dry by the next morning when we planned to set out across the Gulf Stream. Michael and I both have felt that days should be matched with deeds, that good days should be taken advantage of, that auspiciousness is largely a question of good timing. Our symbolic approach to Atlantis-Bimini, therefore, was to be undertaken on the first, pure day of the New Year, the center day of Cayce's prediction. Such a move seemed logical.

However, there are ways and there are ways of reading omens. As it turned out, the weather was not good for crossing. Small craft warnings were posted around noon, winds were up, northeasterly, about 15 to 20 mph, which is worse than it sounds in the Gulf Stream. We were advised not to make the crossing and we didn't. We sat about, instead, as the winds rose, and discussed the idea of our having been sent from Rome to find Atlantis. Such a pastime was pleasant in such weather.

When you bring your boat into a marina and ask for fuel or permission to tie up for the night, the dockmaster says, yes, sir, or yes, Captain. If you are out working on the teak in the stern and someone wishes to attract your attention, he calls you Cap or Captain. You never quite get used to assimilating the layers of tradition and meaning which that name carries with it. It's a bit like getting something for nothing, and for that, it is all the more valuable. On the *Tana* we were both captains, and both of us dealt with the constant decisions that had to be made. We needed all the help we could give to each other.

We each had our particular ways of reaching a decision. Mine was the practical, handbook, if-you-don't-know-ask-somebody-who-does method. Michael combined this with a more or less mystical commune with himself. So if we came to the same decision about something, we could feel certain that both Captain Bligh and someone like Bridey Murphy would concur. And we would either confidently sail or rather smugly resecure our lines.

Our luck with this system cannot be denied. Because the fact is we ran into trouble but never deep trouble. But how many arrows and knives whipped through the air, soundlessly and utterly unnoticed, while we stooped to retrieve a coin or dropped watch? How many crocodile logs missed us by inches, merely for the arbitrary turning of the wheel? How many submerged pilings, and skulking, jagged rocks? We went carefully, yes, and tried to think of everything, but we heard the most fantastic stories from captains about luckless boats, and saw for ourselves enough cow-skull wrecks to make us both think that, in comparison, we were two kids in a tub, atop an immense and vicious, supremely evidential sea.

There was, simply, no other way to go about it. And New Year's Day presented the particularized kind of problem that we, like superstitious, highly unsophisticated Vikings, had to face. There certainly could be no rules for finding the lost continent of Atlantis. It seemed reasonable to approach it emotionally.

If you are heading out to the twin islands of Bimini, which lie forty-two miles due east of Miami, and you follow your compass's 90° heading exactly, you will miss Bimini by seven and a half miles. This is because the Gulf Stream, in which the state of Florida wallows like a pleased hippopotamus, moves northward here at a clip of 2½ knots. And capriciously, this northern set carries everything in and on top of the water along with it, fish and boats alike.

(In writing "the twin islands of Bimini," I have realized that Bimini might be a derivative of Gemini. Further, is Bahama a contraction of Baha Mar?)

You adjust for this northern set by aiming seven and a half miles to the south of Bimini, approaching it on the bias, not approaching it so much as intercepting it. This is a fact that everyone who crosses to Bimini finds out about, usually before it is too late. I mention it now for one reason. If there seems to be nothing between you and your goal, and yet you find you have somehow missed it, the simplicity of your failure can be all the more befuddling. I think it is that way with the concept of Atlantis. Perhaps it is no good at all to approach it directly, logically, or in ways that have been used before, and to questionable avail. No, I think one must approach Atlantis as captains approach Bimini, that is obliquely.

As delicately as I can, let me say that it makes no difference, finally, if the place is ever found, by us or James Mavor and his crowd of Greeks, or by anybody. For its real value lies in its impact as an idea, not as a few rocks, roads or ruined shards. Similarly, it does not matter if it ever existed in the first place. But supposing it did, and supposing we, or somebody else, found it; still, the greater significance of Atlantis might remain hidden or lost. I have read many books related to the Atlantis legend, but I have never come across anything, in any of them, about the ramifications of the place's existence, aside from the usual jabber about crystal walls and Romanesque costumes. Never have I come across an author who could restrain his imagination long enough to consider what it would mean to add a decently evolved civilization to a roster of history that cannot easily accommodate it. Such speculation has been left to science fiction.

90

Further, can there be any real excuse for the presentation of yet another exhumed city? We would all like to know something we did not know before, but we would all be bored, I think, by the prospect of added examples of what we have already put in the backs of our minds as ordinary, if not commonplace. The *Iliad* and the discovery of Troy have taken a lot out of us. We have become jaded by that seven-layered cake of bones. We are waiting for Archaeology to come up with something new, conceptually; to land itself on the moon like everyone else.

Cogently, the Atlantis legend has survived and is popular today because it offers an alternative to the unsatisfying Genesis legend of the Bible. The *deus ex machina* idea carries less conviction in a time when God has been accused of living in Argentina, like Bormann, and when machines, built by ourselves, can do almost anything. I am interested in knowing, more exactly, what was in that bottle labeled "Adam and Eve."

It is necessary to go into this before we get too much further into the forest: I would be embarrassed to write, let alone publish, this account, if we led anyone to believe that we approached this thing or came away from it as instant archaeologists. Our discovery may or may not make an interesting final episode to this book. But I am certainly not going to wait for that to happen. I, at least, did not go off looking for the lost continent of Atlantis. I went looking for the idea of it. Do not expect us to give you golden domes shimmering in the refracted depths. We will be unable to present you with anything but the makings of a rather interesting new diorama for the basement of the Museum of Natural History.

The idea is simple. Can Atlantis have existed? Not, did it,

or when or where; just could it have existed and what does that mean?

To begin with, if Atlantis is an idea, it exists abstractly, in people's minds, and not physically, like a brooch or corsage in the best, most likely spot on a lady's dress. And as an idea it does not exist until it is thought of and discussed, until one mind conceives it and others open themselves up to its significance and true possibilities. Plato conceived the idea. The pages of the *Timaeus* and the *Critias* lie open before us, the famous descriptions shrouded in ambiguity like *Vogue* models—offhandedly, negligently—with a calculated boredom that is near to maddening. But here is the beginning of the idea, the seeds of a weed that has grown for over two thousand years. It is basically incredible, to begin with, that something should last so long without being settled, one way or the other. And why is it that so many "Atlantis's" have been found, and yet the search for it continues? The answer is perhaps very simple. The *idea* of Atlantis has not been found. You do not find an idea beneath the ground or under the sea. And when something is discovered, Atlantean or not, the physical evidence of it is unable to match, in emotional and intellectual impact, the packet of legends and myths which has thrived, above the ground in people's minds, for a millennium.

The Mavor-Galanopolos-Marianatos theory, of Crete, Thera and the Minoan Empire as Atlantis, seems to me more convincing than anything I have ever read or heard about the subject. It is plausible and very well documented. But all those earthquakes, collapsed calderas, tsunamis, all that pumice, death, destruction and resultant ruin say nothing to me about the real significance of Plato's idea; instead it reduces it to something founded on error, ignoring everything the idea has grown into, namely the concept that we, in the present, are perhaps the descendants of a past much older and more glorious than we had imagined, and that our beginnings might have taken place in a garden much larger than Eden. What is disappointing about the Thera-theory is that it insinuates itself into cultural and geological history, with the result that one already important fact of the near past is again underlined. The Atlantean legend has survived and grown for so long because it has been trying to tell us something significant. And the idea will not be laid to rest until a completely new facet of history is exposed, until a new world is uncovered to us. Crete as palimpsest is therefor quite pleasing archaeologically, but inappropriate intellectually. It wraps yet another gaudy ribbon around a package that has been left under the tree too long.

Any combination of northerly or easterly winds has a peculiar and disquieting effect on the Gulf Stream waters off Miami. Even a fifteen-mile-an-hour wind makes them high, nasty and unpredictable, and we waited two days, until January 3, to make the crossing. Small craft warnings were down, but the waters were still up and the three-hour trip was very uncomfortable. I, it must be recorded, embarrassed myself during the middle third and roughest part of the haul, hands on the wheel and head out the wheelhouse window, with a turn to broadside every so often to wash the decks.

We churned across on a compensatory heading of $105°$ to $110°$, emasculating the puffy, prophylactic men-of-war which floated their transparent sacs in our path, un-seeing flying fish that resembled nothing so much as delicate, whirling, model airplanes. The day was overcast and dull. But the sun came out for a bit just as we raised the Bimini

93

light straight off the bow. The water, which had been sodden, sullen and backhandedly gray, took on some color—a very deep blue. Then, quite suddenly, it turned turquoise and transparent just outside the reef. We stopped, a few hundred yards offshore, to take a look around, to turn on the fathometer, to get out the boatmen's Bahama Guide. We were in the lee of the island and the wave action was very low. Just ahead of us the reef lay in about twenty feet of water. Except for the sandy bottom of Biscayne Bay, this was our first look through light, transparent water. And, of course, it was our first reef. We read the instructions for crossing it, looking for a particular casuarina tree landmark on shore. At that moment, looking along the beach through binoculars for the tree, and not seeing it because we were too far north, we were, as nearly as one can now figure, directly over what was later to be our discovery. The dark shapes of it stretched out beneath us on all sides in the twenty-foot-water. At the time they did not register as anything but perhaps a continuation of the reef. Then we saw the channel which separates North from South Bimini, and we put up the throttles and moved away from the dark shapes. A half hour later we were docked in the harbor, in Alice Town, busily washing the salt from the boat, waiting for the customs official to see our yellow quarantine flag and come aboard. It would be a month and a half before the guide, Evangelo, led us back out to the spot where we had first, so inadvertently, stopped the *Tana,* and where, having thought of this first approach to Bimini as symbolic, we had looked all about us, half expecting some immediate proof, which only our fresh objectivity could spot, of this island's specialness, of its bizarre, important history, of its possibilities. Somewhere, we thought, there was a sign, a clue; and yet, despite this feeling, we never had the wit to look down, to remark to each other, or even to ourselves, that those dark shapes which stretched out beneath us had a geometry and order, a peculiar pattern that, unlike a reef, would not make you think of God and nature, but of a lost and ancient race of men.

[9] The ordered layout of the stones is very evident in this photograph. The two white spots are most probably air bubbles.

[10] Count Turolla photographing some of the larger stones.

[11] A close up of the second layer of the stone wall. *(Photo by Renee Turolla)*

[12] In the foreground, the second layer of the wall can be seen. And in the back, a stone disturbed by the 1926 dredging. *(Photo by Count Turolla)*

[13] Sections of a pillar, discovered and photographed by Count Pino Turolla, November 29, 1969, off Bimini, in 15 feet of water.

[14] Different sized pillars are clearly seen. Large pillar showing grooves is five feet in circumference. *(Photo by Count Turolla)*

[15] Group of pillar sections found in underwater floor depression, near an underwater cliff. Sections are between three and five feet in length, and approximately two and a half feet in diameter. *(Photo by Count Turolla)*

[16] Count Turolla tries to lever a large section of a pillar into position for future recovery. *(Photo by Renee Turolla)*

III

Air

The dogs of Bimini are remarkable. On an island otherwise defined by an air of ill will, the three or four dozen animals that live there provide a most comfortable, even obsequious, relief. It is said that every dog on each of the Bahama Islands is the descendant of one great, good-natured bitch brought across the water long ago. How long ago is a question that is, for the most part, unanswerable. In all probability she existed before the period of British rule, which began with the arrival of Governor Woodes Rogers in 1718. And even those dogs which slunk about from settlement to makeshift saloon in the second half of the seventeenth century, accompanying pirates and eel-fishermen, were undoubtedly late descendants of her prodigious womb. From 1492 until 1649 the islands were under Spanish rule, and it may have been at that time that she first arrived, from either the Old World or the New, sauntering down a gangplank with her load of posterity ready to pop. If not, she is far more interesting and

99

far hoarier with antiquity than we can guess; she may have responded to a name that was neither Spanish nor English nor Creole, but pure Mayan. If ever a land bridge existed, as some archaeologists believe it did, between the Yucatan Peninsula and the Islands, she may easily have trotted across it on a Mayan outing and stayed to colonize the scrub forests and coral-sand beaches instead of returning with the rest of her party to the southwestern mainland. In fact, her journey may have been from as far as Ecuador or Peru.

Her exceedingly great-grandchildren, however, bear no witness to such noble beginnings. They inspire little more than pure affection as they raise their always slightly bloated stomachs from the dust roads of Bimini and slowly begin the creaky revolutions of their decidedly ratty tails. They are humble and flea-laden and have refined the doggy art of masochism to a new degree. The ladies allow the ship's dogs from Miami and Pompano Beach to mount them without protestation, smiling foolishly at any intrusion. The males surrender their food to anything vaguely human with a motion somewhere between a cringe and a shudder. They are the essence of hang-dog, hemmed in by the chalky beaches of a tiny island, limited in their diet to an endless procession of conchs and scaly fish. They are scavengers and whores and derelicts, in appearance running from butterscotch to hyena, and we, upon meeting them, loved them all.

While docked at the Big Game Fishing Club, we stepped over and around and through the dogs as they pressed against the sun-warmed hull of *Tana*. They were with us on the streets and in the bars, by day and night that first week, as we tried to sniff out some clue that would direct us somewhere, some bit of information that would reinforce our feeling that Bimini was going to be the place where Atlantis awoke.

In a bar called the Seacrest, to the accompaniment of a jukebox with a fondness for Percy Sledge, we made the acquaintance of a girl named Dikki Tasker and her husband, Robin. They were on Bimini, along with an American agency representative, a German director, and full filming crew, to film an underwater cigarette commercial for European television. Yaria, in Rome, had forecast some connection with television work while on the trip, and so we fell in with them gladly. The next day their filming was delayed because of heavy rains and we all sat about in various places talking about diving and underwater exploration. Because of our association with Margaret and the promise of a rendezvous in February, and because of her warnings about keeping the publicity down on any finds we would make or that had been made, we didn't confide in the Taskers and the rest of their party exactly what we were up to. That we were novelists, that we had taken the boat for the winter as a place to write, that we were interested in underwater exploring, all these things seemed to fit together naturally enough for them; later, when we casually said that we were looking for Atlantis, this too seemed to fit into their pattern of acceptance.

Talking to Robin, and to the director, Andreas, we began to realize that scuba diving wasn't quite as easy as simply falling off a boat. Neither of us, predictably enough, had ever had on an aqualung, nor bothered to do any preparatory reading or practising in indoor pools along the way. That evening Robin gave us the *Scuba Divers Bible* to read. And the next day we dove.

It is a very awkward thing, the first time, to dive. We, who had never before even snorkeled, were suddenly below twenty or thirty feet of water, trying to distinguish between mouth-breathing and nose-breathing, and remembering, above everything else, not to hold our breath. The aqualung, contrary to what I expected from reading Cousteau, is not nearly as natural as one's own; the sound of breathing is magnified as if in stereo, so that it seems every drop of water reflects back into one's already confused ears.

Had we done any preparatory dives or, as everyone is supposed to, played around a bit with the gear in shallow water or a pool, then undoubtedly it wouldn't have been quite so graceless a baptism. Robert, as a matter of fact, did exceedingly well. It was I who inhaled, on first splash, great dollops of salty water through a leaky mask and who knew nothing about the proper number of weights and so would bob toward the surface (the absolutely worst place to be, the most confusing, and the most exasperating with all one's diving armor on) whenever I ceased for a moment kicking myself downward. Our instructor-hosts, Robin and Andreas, were patient and calming and kept filling our belts with more weights and pushing us back under.

The first dive. Even with water slowly filling the mask and the sound of my own breathing filling my head, I eventually relaxed into the contained suspension that all things and bodies underwater partake of. It was a mistake to forego the diving preparations, the question of safety notwithstanding, because those first awkward splashes and little wrinkles of panic took time to smooth out, and by the time I'd shifted down to the right level of movement and balance, my air had quite run out. Robert, meanwhile, was as enthusiastic and natural as a gilled cocker spaniel.

The fish that first day were to us magnificent. There weren't as many as we would see in the next few days on subsequent dives, but they were brilliantly colored—parrotfish in orange and yellow and slivers of indigo, sergeant majors in electric stripes—even the dowdy groupers, less flashy but eminently comfortable, lolling about in the warm current. Bimini is a game-fishing capital, with the bulk of fishing done from above sea level and very little spear-fishing going on below; at least the fish we met seemed to be unconditioned to flee. (Though later, through the separate islands and in various marinas, we met a good many people who did use spear-guns, the idea of introducing that method of underwater killing has always seemed to me slightly gross, rather like firing a shotgun into a tidal pool. But fishing, no matter what the form, has never charmed me; in the five months aboard the *Tana* we never once dropped a line over the side).

That first day we were under for less than half an hour. The television group had their own compressor and a number of tanks, so we were able to go out several times in the next few days before they packed their filming gear and flew to Miami. We found nothing as far as Atlantis was concerned during those first dives, although, with the confidence that comes of total ignorance, we fully expected to discover something monumental each time we went under. Instead, we poked at bits of coral and starfish and got as close as we could to the swarming schools of fish. The last dive together we spent crawling on the ribs and through the rusting bowels of a submerged concrete ship, sister ship to that one which we'd come across our first harbor out in Cape May, New Jersey—the U.S.S. *Atlantis*. It was pleasant, warm, and of itself fascinating; as an omen intriguing, but, as evidence of anything beyond rust, disappointing.

It was necessary for us to leave Bimini and sail to Grand Bahama Island where Robert's parents and aunt had planned a week's vacation, and where we were to meet them with the *Tana*. For that reason we were on the island of Bimini for only the space of time it took us to learn to dive. We left shortly after the television group did, and were able to do no further snooping about the island. In addition to the dives themselves, there had been forays into the coves of neighboring cays, with us picnicking on peanut butter and spareribs on Gun Cay, and being shooed away from the stately but deserted clubhouses and lounges of Cat Cay. We spoke with fewer native Bahamians than we would have liked, and were not really able then to tune into any undercurrent of folk legend that might have guided us to particular sites. But we had, at least, been under the water.

Now, with ears still slightly achey from the dives, we sailed north for Freeport. We stopped only once, to debate anchoring where our charts told us there were rises in the ocean floor of thirty-six and fifty-four feet. The sea was too high, however, and our store of confidence too low, to permit us to do anything more than peer over the side and cluck to one another, like chickens at a mud puddle. We arrived at the Lucayan Marina, said to be the Western Hemisphere's largest, just east of the city of Freeport, and settled into a slip next to a cruiser named *Aquarius III*.

In Freeport we saw no dogs. And the sounds of Bimini, those variations of birdsong that comprise the island dialect, were all but smothered by accents Sicilian and Genovese. Our ears, slightly out of whack anyway, flapped to phrases we had left behind on Via Condotti and Via dei Giubbonari in Rome. The croupiers and dealers moved about in small, gesticulating groups when they were not manning the dice tables in Freeport's large casinos, and everywhere we went we were more aware of Italian being spoken than English, Spanish, or

Bahamese. (Leaving New York and coming down the Waterway to Florida we had of course heard the vowels thickening and the diphthongs beginning to bounce; it was probably in South Carolina and Georgia that American speech condensed into its thickest syrup, to diffuse again as we slid into Florida and Miami Beach. There is a meter to Miami Beach that has little to do with the lilt of palm trees, but even it is flat and undifferentiated compared to the Bahamian line of inflection and stress. Phrases soar upward to feathery peaks unheard in Savannah or on Dade Boulevard, and the meter itself clinks and jangles along like a steel-band locomotive. Each single male voice is an entire chorus, with equal parts soprano, contralto, tenor and bass.) Now, in Freeport, all the scoring seemed to be done in bass clef.

Freeport gets very good press. Unlike Bimini which no one, with the possible exception of Adam Clayton Powell, takes seriously as a pleasure spa—Freeport has a very large number of Doctors Pangloss. There are, they say, the casinos, and the beaches, and the marvelous real estate properties, and the fun opportunities for homogenized swinging, and all the other things that make an otherwise undistinguished stretch of sand and coral and scrub pine an island "paradise." Its promoters compare the island of Grand Bahama and the settlement of Freeport to alternately Tahiti and Monaco, with perhaps a whiff of Capri. The only problem we found with this island built on brain coral was that it had been so lobotomized and reorganized and efficiently done up that any splash of mystery or romance had been rendered as dull as dishwater. Downtown Freeport looks as if it were cast from a plastic mold the night before last. And it looks to have been the same plastic mold that was also used for every shopping center from Menlo Park to Duluth. There is a bust of

Winston Churchill on one small square of lawn, and the cars and little red buses drive on the left-hand side of the road, but aside from these identifying marks the body of Freeport is as anonymous as cream cheese.

There are the casinos. If you don't gamble, casinos are probably the dreariest institutions in existence. If you do, no amount of whining about their vulgarity and tedium is going to matter, and no one will ever be able to convince you that there is probably no such thing as luck, and certainly no such thing as glamour. We spent a lot of time in the casinos, inasmuch as it wasn't very good weather for anything else, and also because there was precious little else to do. There were some revues, where girls with kohl-blackened nipples, and faces and arms bewigged with beret and curls, impersonated with their bodies the faces of one or two famous painters. And a comedy team whose act consisted wholly of ethnic slurs, each against the other. And near the downtown section there was an Italian restaurant, where we were served a nearly poisonous repast, the worst that any of us, and we were five, had ever tasted at any place at any time. (However, the New Hong Kong redeemed the chefs of Freeport with delicate platters of translucent shrimp and glazed pork.) Nights at the casinos were less than scintillating, and the days were filled with clouds, and so Freeport passed, dully, like a gray image on afternoon TV. Freeport was a rerun, and we'd expected, I suppose, something new. (If the entire community of Freeport had been featured at the New York World's Fair five years ago, in the Hall of Enterprise, for instance, I'm sure we would have all enjoyed it immensely.)

We were able to leave, after a false start because of a gummy oil tube the day before, on the twenty-first. As we were pulling away from the Lucayan Marina, two other boats were docking; one of them was the *Amigo del Mar,* and on board was a happy party of moon-bound astronauts enjoying a short reward-cruise. The other boat, a cruiser, had on its deck, in addition to some highly tanned young ladies, a full-grown cheetah sitting with eyes half closed, its muzzle lifted slightly into the wind.

On the voyage across from Grand Bahama to Great Abaco Island, we began to relax and to seemingly spread out a bit in the water. The sunlight was heavy and strong, the seas calm. And looking up, we were able to reacquaint ourselves with, and elaborately fantasize about, the clouds overhead. (I had decided, somewhere north of Georgia on one of those December days we'd passed, with clean nearly brittle clouds striping the pale sky, that clouds are very probably the only gods there are. [If we are made in the image of gods, then this is surely so, for nowhere is the fickle pattern of our thoughts and emotions so well represented as in the motion of curling clumps of energy and vapor across the sky.]) Now, crossing from island to island and heading due east into the morning sun, we were treated to all manner of iconography forming and dissolving above us. As we approached Abaco they clumped low along its toothbrush horizon, and then trailed away completely as we began to enter the shallower water of the harbor. It was low tide and we were forced to slow to nearly no RPMs at all as we did a careful cakewalk across the sandy sea floor dotted with starfish as large as coffee tables and past sandy boulders the size of overstuffed settees. Arriving in the tiny clapboard settlement of Sandy Point, we found a living pace quite different from that of either Freeport or Bimini.

In Sandy Point, the living seemed easy. The two English

teachers we met there, a man and wife team, were proud to show us around their settlement, to point out sharks splashing at low tide in the bay, to describe the attractions of a life only occasionally interrupted by wild boars skittering through their back-yard, or a plague of sand fleas. They maintained a casual and yet efficient relationship with the environment; while their accents were still noticeably British their baby daughter playing on the floor gurgled out pure Bahamese. We were given a tour, and all their pride of territory was reflected in showing us glistening white conch-graveyards and abandoned air strips, and in hallooing gently to various native Bahamians. We joined them for dinner, and after some book talk and some sociology talk, we asked our by then ritualized questions about whether or not they'd heard of any archaeological finds. They hadn't, but would be pleased to keep their ears open. They assured us that as writers we wouldn't find in all the Bahamas a place anywhere nearly as conducive to writing as this, their own settlement, and they politely but sincerely urged us to stay. It was a pleasant and seemingly placid little colony, we decided, having left their clapboard house and commenced groping our way through the inky night on our way back to the *Tana*. But there was a feeling, we agreed, of spectatorship in all that we had seen, rather as if all the elements had been summoned up to a kind of ingratiating attention for us, and even for our hosts, as we passed. It was very like one of the often-repeated "Star Trek" episodes in which Captain Kirk and his crew investigate a strange planet to find there only what they have individually imagined might be there, and nothing else but this kind of subjective manifestation of fantasy.

At the point of making this comparison, however, our reflections came to a rapid halt, as we were suddenly surrounded by a distressingly large number of snarling, yapping island dogs. They seemed to have materialized all at once, and we lit matches to see how many there were, thinking too to frighten them off with the small flames. Bimini had spoiled us with its squadron of hangdogs, and we were therefore both shocked and offended as they chewed at our heels, some twenty or thirty of them. Robert's idea was that if we showed panic, we'd be eaten; mine was that we ought to get the hell out of their territory, whatever it was, and running was the best way to do it. In a compromise shuffle, with a good many savage kicks, we made our way down the dirt road through the dark and finally passed out of whatever range they were defending as we crossed a small rise.

Back upon the *Tana*, we re-established our own floating territory and decided to leave in the morning.

We left Abaco, then, after only a day and a half and arrived in Nassau on the twenty-third of January. The date is memorable to us because, had we arrived even a day earlier, we would have been hard pressed for accommodations. As it was, we were able to arrange billing for our moorage at the Nassau Yacht Haven only because a New York *Times* article on our trip had come out that day, and the woman who either extended credit or sped you on your way was reading it at her desk as we pulled into the marina. It didn't provide us with anything resembling celebrity status, but it did manage to convince her that there was someone else, other than our by-then-grubby selves, responsible for all bills back in New Jersey. And it was a nice coincidence.

By then we were both slightly numbed to the significance of any sort of coincidence; our attitude had progressed to one of quite bland acceptance. After all, it was illogical to believe that every number, color, or name that presented itself to us was an omen, symbol, or harbinger of some colossally trivia-oriented Fate. There had to be some things that "meant" absolutely nothing, otherwise there could be no necessary balance of "significance," and there could be nothing left over for symbols to symbolize or for representations to represent. The whole concept of symbology is a thorny one when it comes to the Occult Plane; if one is not highly selective, one is soon plagued by swarming droves of symbols, all arranged in the most maddeningly reinforcive order, but all merely buzzing and occasionally stinging one's fingers, but never really explaining a damned thing. It is a dicey business to snatch significance from the jaws of omen-overload. It is far easier to let oneself be consumed whole and find one's sensibilities thereby a digested pap of non-discrimination. The end result of such a process is the sort of thing that happens when acid-heads drop too many sugar cubes; every aspect of existence means something so profound that no explanation is adequate to define its mysteries, and so no effort toward explanation or further clarification is made. One sits and simply grooves. Or one simply sits.

(Probably, of course, everything ultimately has a contextual significance; and everything perceivable shares a relationship with its perceptor that is signifiable. The real question though is whether the symbol for that relationship is anything more intriguing than a function of that particular relationship. In matters occult, this symbol function seems too often to be given more importance than the form it describes, and such a "Behaviorism of Symbology" seems to be the most cherished of all topics of discussion. In and about the flanges of the psychic community there now and again crop up ladies and gentlemen, on lecterns and in seminars, whose smugness of smile and speech reflects their belief in secret symbols as ends in themselves. Adding up the number of times such and such a symbol has occurred in a particular doxology a flushed and self-important matron will exhibit the sum total as if it were, in and of itself, infinitely more important than whatever truth or quality it represents. And then she will lower her voice and perhaps close her eyes, as if to keep all but the knowing away from her own plump body of secret knowledge. The idea of necessary secretude is really a bore; symbols ought to be considered a means of making certain truths more obvious, rather than more obscure. Symbols, no matter how attractive, are still only media, and to say that they are more important than the message behind them is to negate form completely for the sake of its function.)

I believe in symbols—it is virtually impossible not to, and still cope with the world—but I do not believe in all symbols, nor in the existence of only symbols. It is just as I believe that certain books are valid and true representations of reality but do not believe that all books are valid, or that there is nothing more to reality than books (no matter how attractive that idea may sometimes seem). Up to this point in our trip, Robert and I had sucked in omens and coincidences like whales harvesting plankton; perhaps with this last little fillip of coincidence about the *Times* article we had become stuffed to the bursting point, and, somewhere along our corporate dorsal fin, there was beginning to blink, in water-resistant neon, the word, Tilt.

The sun shone nearly every minute of every day we spent in Nassau. Or so it now seems. We settled down to a routine of waiting and writing which extended through the second of February, when we sailed back across the Grand Bahama Bank for Bimini and Miami. The waiting was for some word from Margaret and M.A.R.S. about the convocation we had all talked about, we were not sure whether it would take place on Bimini or Andros and so were anxious to know which direction to start in. The writing was the beginning scratches of each our second novel: Robert would spend the morning typing in the galley or working out notes in the wheelhouse, while I sat in one of the stern fishing chairs, typewriter propped against the gunnel. The atmosphere at the marina was easy to work in; there were few distractions during the day, and at night there was nothing so attractive it demanded late attendance. There seemed to be nothing around to smoke, and drinking at the tourist bars was a bit expensive, so we bided our time in sunny sobriety until the wire arrived from Margaret announcing, in scrambled-egg phrases sprinkled with intrigue, that we would all be convening on Bimini.

The winds were too choppy to leave until the morning of the second. Then the water unwrinkled and the early morning harbor provided us a flat runway out onto the sea. We slid across the Bank without incident until the port engine began rasping and wheezing, and we were faced with our first mechanical complication. This, it later turned out, was due only to a lack of proper grade transmission oil, but at the time we were as concerned at the sound and change in respiration as if one of our own lungs had suddenly ceased to function. We held down our speed and crossed the remainder of the Bank using only the starboard engine, and were thereby forced to enter the shallow channel and reef-studded approach to Cat Cay, and then Bimini, at dusk. We managed to so navigate without any mishap, creeping at a sea-slug's pace into Big Game Fishing Club as the last trace of bluish-pink quit the sky.

And there we sat, unfortunately, for four days while high winds and white water filled the channel and the marina, unable to leave for Miami, as a local mechanic advised us, to have whatever a "dog-shaft" was, located and installed. The winds were up to twenty-five knots for those days, and the nights cold and black; we wrote a bit and waited. On the fourth day we were able to rise in the morning without having to secure the coffee pot firmly to the stove; the winds had died and the sea was down, and we eased our ailing engines out into the channel and over the Gulf Stream with a kindly southeastern moving softly behind us. By twelve o'clock we had delivered *Tana* into the surgical hands of Miami Beach Yacht Corporation, and ourselves into the equally rehabilitative arms of M.A.R.S. The next day we lunched with Margaret, and also Marguerite, who had flown in a few days before, over chopped liver and cheese cake supplying each other with our respective comings and goings for the time elapsed. (Margaret had been attending presidential inaugurations, fainting dead away she was sorry to have to confess, at the inaugural ball, in a rather spectacular gold sari.) (Marguerite had been dropping in on people in Canada and the Far West, treating all of North America as if it were really no larger or more difficult to get around than Dorset or Sussex county.)

We were pleased beyond measure to be in their company, now we could listen to cleanly articulated flights of probability and possibility that were as entertaining as they were edifying, and begin to identify, by their repetition, certain names which represented particular varieties of divination and mystical understanding. Everything seemed to be pointing toward an archaeological excursion later in the month in which all our skills, both seafaring and psychic, would be put to use. Names occurred in conversation that, with each mention, took on added detail, until, when we were finally introduced, the models themselves were no more or less fascinating than their by then highly embroidered portraits.

Ever since Rome, where we had first encountered the glassy-eyed stare that tells you, in no uncertain terms of expression, that you are being regarded as an insane and therefore slightly dangerous animal, we had done our best to avoid casting such a glance ourselves. Inasmuch as such a glance draws its hostility more from fear than pure malice, it also perhaps reflects the assumption that sanity is far less dangerous than insanity to all citizens of logic and good will. I am not at all sure I share that basic assumption, thinking, rather, that what we call "sanity" is only an arbitrary fencing off of certain areas of thought and action which we mustn't gambol about in, lest we turn into catatonic toads. I think that such a gambol may instead give us the means to deal more knowledgeably with our own fate, and that a little insanity ought to be relished by the best of men. It undoubtedly and most frequently is. However, there is no arguing with the fact that most outside opinion would have labeled us, could that opinion have seen us and listened to us as we planned our excursion, True and Certifiable Crazies, one and all. There were so many holes in our timetable, and gaps in the network of our theories, that our only possible method of operation was a reinforcement of each the other's private stock of theories. In that way all of us hung together, swinging back and forth in that period of time, fastened by the same tenuous thread.

There is something to be said for the manner with which all crazies, be they fully accredited or not, respectfully treat one another. One sees them giving full and concentrated attention to each other's mutterings on park benches from Hyde Park to Union Square. Gray brows are knitted and thin lips drawn together as the sympathetic strain among them alternates with the passionately articulate. The full homage of critical attention is paid to private and intricately convoluted theories which are carried about from bench to bench like those bags, also seen in public parks, filled with odd bits of fruit, peanut shells, and handfuls of faded confetti. The respect is gentle and reassuring, the confetti is handled with care, and there is a chivalrous formality in the ritual of change from speaker to listener. In a small tribe of old men, gathered together on park benches on a mall, there are no hypotheses, only pure facts, and in such a convocation of pure brilliance, there is no real discord. (Novice crazies, those pretenders-to-madness, are in a different category altogether, falling in an aggressive limbo that recommends them to neither the dotty nor the dull.) But these ashen old men, bowing toward one another like great frazzled Kabuki dolls, perhaps know that madness is the natural state of man, and so treat that nature to a sense of grace. There are so many far less attractive things to be than merely mad—greedy, say, or insensitive—that in comparison these crazies seem both sweet and kind. It is only when they are brought into contact with the world beyond the park mall that they become grotesque.

For the next week or so, we were kept busy bowing and tipping our various hats to the people behind the names which Margaret and Marguerite had mentioned. One afternoon we sat munching on Girl Scout cookies and sunflower seeds in one of the rooms of the pastel villa Margaret had taken as M.A.R.S. headquarters on Hibiscus Island, meeting for the first time an agreeable young British journalist with five names, hyphens scattered among them; Margaret's own son, pilot Trigg; another pilot, Bob Brush, who had made the first sighting of the "temple" off Andros that we had read about in the Rome *Daily American* before leaving Italy; and the man who'd done all the theorizing in the article, Dr. Manson Valentine. We all listened, along with Dr. Valentine's wife, Ann, and Margaret's daughter, who happened to drop in, to the sounds of a mockingbird in the garden. Dr. Valentine would listen quite intently for a bit, and then announce the bird which the mockingbird was emulating. This led us for some reason to talk of bower-birds, and others, and to listen with interest as Dr. Valentine explained how the cuckoo lays her eggs to resemble those of the nest she chooses to house them. It was a polite and learned discourse, and Robert and I were impressed with the doctor's knowledgeability of these strange birds.

Another day the ladies brought over to the now repaired *Tana* a psychiatrist who wished to be included on the excursion and who was extremely well acquainted with Cayce, and the business of dream interpretation. We all went off together to outfit Dr. Hotchkiss with the necessary weight belts and mask apparatus, plus tank and fins, preparing him for any underwater eventuality. After that we and the gear rode out to Dinner Key where Margaret had decided we would all lunch with an old friend of hers whom she'd run into at the opera (*Faust*) the night before. The old friend turned out to be the wife of an American writer living in Rome. Robert and I had been pleased to meet them both at a publishing party while we lived there, and it was an odd line of acquaintance, we all agreed, that had arranged for us to meet again. There were that day many photographs looked at, Alice's of Rome, and Margaret's just developed of some previous outings on Bimini. This rather improbable mixing of conversation and locale lasted through the afternoon, until it was time to call at the home of Dr. Valentine for more specialized topics of conversation.

It was the first time that the Drs. Hotchkiss and Valentine met one another, and the former seemed to be completely charmed by the latter. We leafed through UFO information while nibbling at tiny saucers of flan and then, sometime around six o'clock when we were beginning to clamor for Dr. Valentine to show us his archaeological slides, the electricity suddenly failed. In the dark, then, with only an occasional candle being lit and soon expiring, we continued our exhortations toward the doctor and his wife to be allowed to see those slides which illustrated his theories of a unified prehistory of man. He seemed to be reluctant to show us anything at all until he was given the assurances of the ladies and ourselves that he was to be included, for sure, on the *Tana* party. (He felt, with what was justifiable cause, that he was in a certain amount of disfavor with the board of M.A.R.S. because of his past little dances into the limelight with what were the Society's discoveries. The limelight itself was the distressing factor; it was a question of any publicity given to relatively unexplored finds as being potentially dangerous to those finds, and also the manner in which such information had been leaked.) Margaret assured Dr. Valentine that there could be no thought of such an exploration of Bimini without him, and, apparently well satisfied with this assurance, he began shuffling his slide trays in the dark. When the lights blinked back on, we all smilingly shared the authoritative glow of his discourse as various icons from various cultures clicked past on the screen and a brief explanation of derivation was given to each. After the slides his wife served tea, and there were some further explanations of different codes of symbology, all implicitly but never directly being referred to as purely Atlantean in nature. We talked of different aspects of Atlantis. We talked, for instance, about clothes.

In the Cayce readings on Atlantis, and even in Plato's *Critias,* the mention of clothing is slight. The body of Atlantis fiction generally credits the tailors of the culture with a fondness for swag and flow; the pages of most such speculative novels rustle and swish with the movements of robed high priestesses at the altar. But the actual processes of fashion are seldom gone into; there may have been looms or there may not have been. The materials which fashioned their garments may have been natural or man-made, their gowns given to fitted bodices as well as spaghetti straps, their hems as fashionably mini as maxi. Or the question of fashion may have been completely moot, with the ladies and gentlemen of Atlantis wearing nothing at all.

This last possibility seems a bit remote, inasmuch as a culture which so respected the particulars of existence must surely have incorporated those particulars into their clothing. If stones and gems and colors were used for healing and maintaining a certain energetic equilibrium, then it would seem natural for clothing to be used as a means of keeping those very vibrations continually close to the body. Clothes may well have "made the man," with their vibrations insuring him a very real physical security (the type of security which today derives more from a bulletproof vest than from a Cardin sports jacket). The weavers of Atlantis may well have woven, not with the hair color and eyes of their subject in mind, but rather with the dates and number of his birth, in that way reinforcing the particular physical rhythm going on within his particular body. Clothes as symbols of status would be a post-Atlantean digression, with the real function of wardrobe being something with which twentieth century man is only in subconscious touch. The different energy quotients of materials as dissimilar as fiberglass and mink—the different speeds, for instance, at which their atoms bounce—may explain more concerning their different appeals than does their relative scarcity on the market. And the appeal of certain colors for certain people may today be explainable more in terms of the complementary vibrations these colors produce than in terms of the more acceptable theory of color aesthetics. Even the heightened vulnerability of a naked body is perhaps as much a matter of the vulnerability of a reduced energetic force-field as it is a matter of exposure to the physical and psychological weather surrounding it.

Whatever the ramifications of Atlantean wardrobe are, one of them is, obviously, that their clothes were not, in the final analysis, protection enough. In the Bible, Joseph's robe of many colors may have helped him to ward off the dangers of the pit into which he was later cast by his brothers, but apparently no such mixing of hue and fabric was able to gainsay the nuclear and volcanic destruction with which the equally stalwart of Atlantis were finally faced. Either by their own hands, or owing to some extraterrestrial decision, they were as a culture wrapped in the metaphorical robe of Medea, and, even as they preened, were consumed.

The idea of costume as culture-indicator is an intriguing one; an extension of it is the notion that the clothes one wears, personal energy vibrations for the moment aside, are solid clues to past incarnations. Whether a man wears loose boxer shorts, or prefers tightly knit briefs, may indicate his former costume as either a togaed Roman or a securely trussed

Renaissance man. Those young ladies who choose bra-lessness today may be harking back to a more familiar Minoan ethic, while their mothers prefer a more severe and crisply ruffled Elizabethan look. Some today prefer to wear the costume which represents their most pleasant incarnation-memory. Some prefer to wear them all, and all at once. (There is a young lady in Manhattan, a fully accredited Jewish American Princess of the highest stock and breeding who, in her appearance and costume, represents the whole of history. Both at social gatherings and in her own salon, she displays herself with a mixture of period and gesture that inspires affinity in a variety of races and cultures. To begin with, her hair is a dark chestnut mane that, when it is ornamented with ivory combs and hairpins, might easily have graced the head of a Japanese concubine a thousand years ago. The features of her face complement the oriental inclination of her head, and the gold and silver ornaments she frequently wears about her neck stretch the particulars of her previous appearances across the width of all of Asia. About her breasts and arms the sheerest silks are hung, with fine and intricate patterns of woven flowers, over these are worn cashmere sweaters and knitted shawls with such grace as to suggest a decorous and slightly drafty middle-European appearance. Her robes are Guatemalan prints and geometrical Indian patterns, about her waist is tied a crimson sash with tiny Persian bells sewn along its border. And on her legs, all-American limbs that boast the rounded calf of the nubile college girl, are great fur boots that might have walked with dignity through the winter palace in St. Petersburg a century or two past. So she sits at her loom or her library desk on Central Park West, attended by a loping Great Dane and her wardrobe of memories; an exquisite picture book, her body a testament to karmic beauty and grace.)

Clothes we talked about, and sometimes drugs (neither Margaret nor Marguerite could see the benefits of marijuana), and Egyptology, and many aspects of a belief in reincarnation. One subject which we never pursued for any period of time was one with which, ideally, we all ought to have been knowledgeably familiar. This was the matter of continental drift, ocean plates, and the academic opinion that there was, quite simply, no room for Atlantis in the Atlantic because Africa and America had once been one in that very spot.

Geophysical evidence indicates that there was no Atlantic Ocean at all some one hundred fifty million years ago. In the Lower Paleozoic, a period of time which stretched from 650 million to 400 million years ago, there was an ocean where the Atlantic now lies, traceable today in the sediments of the Caledonian- Hercynian- Appalachian mountains of Europe and North America. But this ocean was drained and dry long before the present Atlantic Ocean appeared, and in the time between the two, Africa, Europe, and North and South America all theoretically bunched together, their coastlines neatly locking like pieces of a gigantic jigsaw puzzle, in the area where the ocean had been and would again be. What eventually pushed these huge land masses apart was the motion of enormous land "plates" moving away from one another, beneath the continents, as the result of ridges spreading and respreading on the ocean floor. As the polar axis changed, these ridges were influenced by that shift, as were the "continental plates" which moved in reaction to them.

In the Cayce readings, the earliest date mentioned concerning any type of Atlantean civilization or culture is one 10,500,000 years old. In reading 5748–2, Cayce records:

The Courts which were made were in the tents and the caves of the dwellers of the then chosen priest from the Arabian or Tibetan country, who came as one among those, to assist with the astrologer and the soothsayer of the desert of now the eastern and western worlds; and with this the conclave was held for many, many moons. The period in the world's existence from the present time being ten and one-half million (10,500,000) years, and (in) the changes that have come in the earth's plane many have risen in the lands. Many lands have disappeared, many have appeared and disappeared again and again during these periods; gradually changing as the condition became to the relative position of the earth with the other spheres through which man passes in this solar system.

These changes in the "relative position of the earth with the other spheres" can easily refer to such a change in the earth's polar axis, a change which occurred again and again as the earth moved through the later Miocene, the Pliocene, and into the notably zany Pleistocene.

Matching up dates in these great chunks of historical time is at best an arbitrary business. It would be convenient if those dates which Cayce assigns to the three major cataclysms of Atlantis—50,700 B.C., 28,000 B.C., and the last of approximately 10,000 B.C.—all coincided with periods of axis shift and continental spreading. It would be equally helpful if there were some cause and effect theory that posited and documented a more than casual relationship between the first mentioned date in the readings, some 10,500,000 years ago, and the change from Miocene to Pliocene at that time.

But the room for error and conjecture is so great as to make educated guesses seem remarkably flimsy; any coincidence of polar switch, interplanetary bounce, and continental squeeze has to be theorized only in the wraps of pure speculation.

The works of Immanuel Velikovsky include intriguing theories of intraplanetary magnetism and the causes of cataclysmic disasters. The idea that a change in the inclination of the terrestrial axis is the result of the earth's entrance into a strong magnetic field is an idea that begins to explain how and why the climatic zones on earth were changed. The so-called cataclysm theory of Cuvier, when it was advanced in 1827, maintained that species and genera were unchanged since Creation, but that there had occurred certain global catastrophes which annihilated large portions of existing life, and these annihilated forms were replaced with new forms. The new forms were never explained to Cuvier's own satisfaction; he theorized that they either arrived from undisturbed parts of the earth or else were newly created. But his theory of sudden catastrophe was not in alignment with the theory of gradual evolution which Lamarck was then teaching, and which Darwin later refined, of evolution proceeding in a rather sleepy trek across tens of thousands of years, uninterrupted by all but the most gradual of geological changes. Cuvier, and DeLuc before him, espoused a theory which did not fit into the over-all masonry of evolution, one which did not maintain, as did that of Lyell, Lamarck, and Darwin, that forces which were not demonstrably operative in the nineteenth and twentieth centuries had not been operative previously in geological time. That seems a rather silly exclusivity now, but it is a principle on which the wall of evolutional theory rests, even today.

The right angles described by scientific theories and

countertheories through the years are matters of considerable complexity. This complexity perhaps explained our reluctance to pursue, even among ourselves, the lines of scientific speculation which various theories of global change and upheaval demanded. If we once began an inquiry based on any particular theory, we were obliged to see it through, and such a speculative journey demanded more allegiance to scientific research than any of us were then prepared to give. The specifications of Cayce's readings and predictions were quite particular enough, we felt, even though they encompassed acres of open water, and even though they advised as guidelines only those clues which popped up to each of us on a thoroughly non-scientific and completely subjective network. We continued to consult the readings, and to read in early ARE publications what might turn out to be helpful psychic data contributed by various psychics concerning where, precisely, to look. Bimini was not the only place where Atlantean artifacts were said to exist; in other Cayce readings the following observations are made:

Reading 364–3: The position the continent Atlantis occupied is between the Gulf of Mexico on one side and the Mediterranean on the other. Evidences of Atlantean civilization may be found in the Pyrenees and Morocco and in British Honduras, Yucatan, and parts of the Americas— especially near Bimini and in the Gulf Stream in this vicinity.

Reading 440–5: . . . As indicated, the records as to ways of constructing same (a large cylindrical glass) are in three places in the earth, as it stands today: in the sunken portion of Atlantis, or Poseidia, where a portion of the temples may yet be discovered under the slime of ages of sea water— near what is known as Bimini, off the coast of Florida.

And (secondly) in the temple records that were in Egypt, where the entity acted later in cooperation with others towards preserving the records that came from the land where these had been kept. Also (thirdly) the records that were carried to what is now Yucatan, in America, where these stones (which they know so little about) are now—during the last few months—being uncovered.

In Yucatan there is the emblem of same. Let's clarify this, for it may the more easily be found. For they will be brought to this America, these United States. A portion is to be carried, as we find, to the Pennsylvania State Museum. A portion is to be carried to the Washington preservation of such findings; or to Chicago.

(This last reading, the portion of it quoted here, was made in 1933. Whether those discoveries made in Yucatán which are here predicted were, in fact, carried out or whether they are still to be made and carried to those places named, I do not know.)

Because we were bound to investigate the Bimini prediction, because there were actual dates mentioned concerning that prediction, and because we had been led so nicely to Bimini itself and to the organizational means to facilitate the search, we focused our attention on finding what there was to find only in Bahamian waters. If, however, we had come upon our interest in Atlantis earlier or later in time, and had had both a wealth of time and money to pursue leads in any and all directions, I do not think we could have long resisted running off to Egypt. The Cayce clues on what is awaiting discovery there are, to me, wonderfully tempting: Egyptology is fascinating in and of itself, and with the added intrigue of an Atlantean thread running through its already rich culture, the prospect of poking about the pyramids is a hugely appealing one.

Reading 3575–2: . . . in Egypt, of the Atlanteans who set about to preserve records—(the entity) came with those groups who were to establish the hall of records or house of records and may directly or indirectly be among those who will yet bring these to light.

Reading 378–16: The entity Hept-supht led in keeping of the records and buildings that were put in their respective places . . . at this time.

This was in the period, as given, of 10,500 years before the entering of the Prince of Peace in the land, to study to become an initiate in or through those same activities that were set by Hept-supht in this dedication ceremony. . . . (In a sealed room there contained) a record of Atlantis from the beginning of those periods when the Spirit took form, or began the encasements in that land; and the developments of the peoples throughout their sojourn; together with the record of the first destruction, and the changes that took place in the land; with the record of the sojournings of the peoples and their varied activities in other lands; and a record of the meetings of all the nations or lands, for the activities in the destructions that became necessary with the final destruction of Atlantis; and the building of the pyramid of initiation; together, with whom, what, and where the opening of the records would come, that are as copies of the sunken Atlantis. For with the change, it (the temple) must rise again.

In position this lies—as the sun rises from the waters—as the line of the shadow (or light) falls between the paws of the Sphinx; that was set later as the sentinel or guard and which may not be entered from the connecting chambers from the Sphinx's right paw until the time has been fulfilled when the changes must be active in this sphere of

126

man's experience. Then (it lies) between the Sphinx and the river.

Reading 519–1: . . . in Egypt during the building of many tombs that are being found today (the entity) aided in the construction of the Hall of Records yet to be uncovered.

Nowhere have I found any instructions as to when these records of Atlantis will be found; in all the Cayce readings there is nothing which resembles the pinpointing of discovery, as in the case of Bimini in either 1968 or 1969. And so they may be under investigation at this very moment, or there may be no excavation for another decade. It would seem, though, that the mushrooming interest in Cayce and the psychic world would be reflected in more serious exploration of those areas he deemed worthy of interest. But perhaps this is not necessarily the case. People connected with the Institute and ARE are forever going on about the necessity for the time being "right." Without the time being right, they say, no amount of exploration or effort is going to come up with anything more interesting than the bones of a few mad dogs or stray Englishmen. Egypt will wait, it seems, until circumstances not only allow, but arrange, the records contained there to be revealed. For Bimini, however, such is not the case. Cayce himself had wound up the clock of that particular prediction, and now, with over half the total hours elapsed, the time, according to his specifications was, most decidedly, "right."

In talking with Margaret, and Lloyd Hotchkiss, and in letting our various theories on dreams and their importance run like hungry white mice through the maze of attempted interpretation, our ideas may or may not have benefited from the exercise. Undoubtedly our social compatibility did. And, probably, we were able to help one another along, if ever so slightly, each toward his own code of personal dream-shorthand. There are, it was generally decided, dreams. And then there are Dreams. In the first category there is the sort of sensory finger painting that the mind itself does, perhaps to amuse itself, perhaps out of something like boredom merely playing with the elements at hand. The following is a dream dreamed somewhere on the Waterway coming down to Florida, somewhere cold, where it was necessary for me to sleep very close to the electric heater all night.

I am on a great gray planet, somewhere far from earth, which has been singed by a passing meteorite or otherwise burned by fire. I witness a party of VIPs come on a diplomatic mission from some other planet, approaching the inhabitants of this one. They are greeted by a young lady, human, who resembles no one so much as Veronica Lake; her hair falls forward, completely obscuring one side of her face as she smilingly greets the visitors. It is all a ruse however—besides Veronica, there are other stewardess-types who, heads tilted and similarly obscured, come out in welcome—but I am able to see, whereas the VIPs are not, that each of them has her face burned purple and swollen beneath the hair."

Between such an obvious dream, and an actual Dream, there is a category of experience which might be either. It is the sort of experience that one never knows how to interpret correctly, as in the case of the following:

In some sort of Egyptian surroundings, witnessing a sort of documentary film on mummification and the soul. Two caskets, pink, appear before a kind of altar; before them a candle burns. The two caskets are touching, having been placed closely together, and as the soul escapes, the candle before them expires. I, watching, wear turquoise and gold jewelry—a necklace and a thin band about my waist. I also have on a smaller, tighter collar, around my neck. The two souls seem to be one.

It's possible that such a dream as the above is a valid flashback, a karmic regression, to an earlier lifetime. Had it not occurred so vividly, though, I would probably have had no trouble at all ascribing it to my interest in the Cayce readings on Egypt. The first dream of Veronica Lake I had because I slept with my face close to a heater, this second one I may or may not have had because I had spent time in Egypt, and it was, if so, post-cognitive. The third type of dream, though, a proper Dream, I had because I was going to discover Atlantis. It showed me what form that discovery would take at a time—the night before we were all to leave for Bimini—when I had really no precise idea of what we were looking for.

Huberia, or a name very similar; a section of country or country itself in which I am in the process of some sort of excavation-discovery. With me are my father and my son, and the three of us are employed at the task of raising, by a series of long thick ropes, what appears to be a very large brown encrusted rectangle or stone slab. It is extremely heavy, and seems to have been buried somewhere. We are in a hall or auditorium, and as we adjust the ropes, the opinion of those gathered around us in the really very large hall is that what we are doing is the opposite of what we have been expected to do. In other words, we are either lowering the slab when everyone expects us to raise it, or we are raising it when we've been expected to lower it. It is slightly confusing, but we manage, by our efforts, to do that which we've decided to do, whichever it is. The audience which observes us may well be in some sort of a church.

A brown encrusted slab. I didn't run hooting down the corridors of M.A.R.S. the next morning with my dream diary tightly in hand, simply because the image of a brown slab was thoroughly uninteresting to me. At that point we all, I think, secretly pictured golden amphorae and great sculptured goddesses waiting for us beneath the sand; it was not especially exciting to think that there would be no intricately detailed and splashy hieroglyphics to decipher, nor smiling Atlantean artifacts to disentangle from centuries of coral and perhaps volcanic encrustation. No, as the final object of our search, as the goal toward which we had all been so obliquely heading, the brown slab simply would not do. After writing out the Dream the next morning, then, I promptly and completely repressed it. And went about, with Robert and Margaret, Dr. Valentine and Marguerite and Lloyd, preparing the *Tana* for crossing, laying in supplies of food and drink, leafing through ARE newsletters, and, every so often, lifting my nose to the psychic wind, hoping, along with everyone else, to catch some signal, some omen on the breeze, that would tell us all to hesitate no longer.

That last day in Florida, before we left for Bimini, was filled with a myriad of tiny chores, and we all, having decided that we ought to leave the next day, omens or no, went our separate detail-filled ways. Before picking up yoghurt, skim milk, and pickled herring at the Food Fair, I made a last little foray through Miami Beach, collecting there two small incidents which raised my spirits oddly.

The first occurred in an Orange Julius stand on Collins Avenue. Walking in and seating myself at the counter, I am waited on by a particularly attractive young waitress who begins to take my order with a great deal of smiling charm. It is a warm day, and the top few buttons of my shirt are unbuttoned, it is as warm for the young waitress who wears an equally open neck, and, as we mutually charm each other over an order of papaya juice, our eyes as mutually find each other's bared necks. There, around hers, hangs a small zodiac medallion which bears her sun sign, a female archer, Sagittarius. Around mine there hangs my own sign, Cancer. We notice each the other's at precisely the same moment, and in the moment realize the futility of any further flirtation. The two of us each cool and, with a brief look say with our eyes all there is to say about the inadvisability of any continuance of contact. We both straighten, my glass of juice is brought with no further grace, and she scribbles quite unlovingly the amount of my bill across her pad and walks briskly away.

Walking back to the supermarket, then, I encountered vignette number two. Along one of the side streets of the Beach, with its look-alike vacation hotels on either side, there appears a knot of quite elderly people standing, together and apart, at the grass lined curb. There is some quarreling and some nervous laughing, all in all the atmosphere is one of general impatience; a few of their number from time to time step carefully into the street and look up its length. At last, as I stand watching, they all press happily forward and from their tightened fists produce pieces of small change. Drawing up in front of them is an obviously late Good Humor truck, and as the driver hastens to fill their orders, he is surrounded by their harangue. Some are less good-natured than others, but, as the last of them receives his ice cream bar and makes his way back to the squadron of painted lawn chairs where everyone sits, there is a feeling of great good fellowship among them all, and the unmistakable aura of youth.

Back on the boat, Lloyd has brought over his newly bought scuba gear and is tucking it away with a somewhat baroque affability. We learn that Dr. Valentine will not be able to accompany us on the ride across, preferring instead to fly over by himself once the rest of us have arrived. Consulting Margaret and Marguerite, we decide there is no reason to wait until the following morning to cross, and instead plan a casting-off for sometime after midnight.

At two o'clock that next morning we receive the ladies and Lloyd aboard and interpret the balmy weather forecast as sufficient sign that both our separate heads and the over-all time are "right." Pulling out of the Yacht Corporation, we pass away from the still-blinking lights of Miami Beach and Miami on either side, and out into the darker night beyond. Both the sea and sky darken as we pass the channel buoys; looking up we are surprised and disappointed to see above us a night completely bereft of stars.

IV

Earth

I

We crossed at night, huddled over the panel lights on the bridge as if over a warming fire. The trip seemed badly timed for the lack of moon and stars, but the sea was abstracted and indolent and then, for the most part, forgetful and flat. We crossed slowly. We would reach the Bimini reef at dawn, which came about six, if not slightly before. In the meantime, and as if to make up for the incompetent stars, the water was evanescent with plankton. And we looked a bit for darker shapes, whales feeding, expecting them to loom along the horizon like ships; and I remember one of us said he had once been able to write his name incandescently in the sand along the high-water mark, though he had had to write very fast to have all the letters of his name glow at once. It was perhaps Lloyd who said that, though, on second thought, I can't easily associate him with such poetics. He, Michael and I were up on the bridge. Michael smelled jasmine or honeysuckle on the wind. Behind us the lights of Miami were a buffer. Margaret and Marguerite had lain down in the bow bunks, below, soon after starting out. I saw them in my mind as twin figureheads of the *Tana's* luck. We picked up the Bimini beacon and crossed the reef at first light, passing a sailboat run hard aground on the bar. Her lights were still on and we could see two people crawling on the listing deck. We stopped to ask if they needed help, but they did not. They were manning her against salvagers. It was full light when we docked in Alice Town.

I remember that when I was first in Italy, visiting my mother's family, I had a great deal of trouble communicating with them. This difficulty seemed compounded by the fact that I had command of enough of the language to make myself comfortable, but not enough of it to be properly understood. As a result, I was not continually informed as to the choreography of my stay there. I was taken about the city and shown to the various members of the family as I guess I would show a new puppy to my friends. There was no lack of politeness in this. There was simply no way of explaining to me that Zia Angelina was waiting to see me, that the ice cream at a certain shop in town was world famous, that the view from a certain hill was a must for visitors. I went along and learned to make the proper noises. And if I was a bit bewildered by it, at least my hosts were pleased.

It was this way with Michael and me for most of the five-day expedition on Bimini. One was not always kept informed. Though I think that this was because no one knew exactly where he stood in relation to what was going on. Indeed, what *was* going on? Margaret and Marguerite knew, I think, only slightly more than we did, though this was not always obvious. Lloyd seemed only to be waiting for his wife to arrive, and when she did, things became a bit better defined. (That definition having to do largely with the fact that she brought with her, quite unexpectedly, three of her friends, as well.) The great enigma, Dr. Valentine, seemed the key to it all and he appeared not to be interested in explaining anything to anybody. He answered all direct questions wryly or wandered off into abstracts and tangential trivia that were maddeningly irrelevant. At first we thought that in our complete ignorance we were asking the unanswerable. Certainly he gave us the impression that not having taken the prerequisite archaeology courses, we stood no chance of understanding the payoff seminar. The lecturer was not entertaining questions at this time. We would do better to take copious notes.

The sense of being included in a common mission being absent, there was nothing to unite us, as, more intelligently, there should have been. Very strangely, considering the trouble we had taken to get there with the *Tana,* our motives were questioned by everyone except Margaret and Marguerite, but especially by Valentine. He told us nothing because he wished us to know nothing. But at the time, that suited us perfectly. I was interested primarily in the people we had fallen in with, and only secondarily with the possibility that we might find Atlantis. We did not have, at the time, any idea that this book would ever be written, and would not know for another four months. But perhaps it was obvious that we were fascinated by what we were doing. And I'm sure we had about us the ulterior look of those taking mental notes. Michael and I realized immediately that we were living future prose, in one form or another, and perhaps Valentine mistook our concern as writers for that of serious fortune hunters. That is the best one can do in terms of hindsight.

Margaret, Marguerite, Michael, and I talked frequently of the problems of personality that surrounded us, and of the need to sublimate all to the goals of the expedition; we must forestall polarization at all costs. But these conversations, which only added to our already substantial *esprit de corps,* probably did more than anything to achieve what we had so earnestly meant to avoid. The others sensed immediately that we were bound up in some sort of agreement, and they automatically and paranoiacally surmised it to be one of deception. And so very early on, two groups were formed, with two levels of communication between them—the polite, ostensibly co-operative, comradery of new friends, and the dark, rather conniving, intuitive, comic-terrifying attitude of the would-be psychic. This dichotomy probably would have been easy (and fascinating) enough to cope with, except that Dr. Valentine was not a member of either group. This was, in fact, the basis of the rivalry. There were ten of us all together, and I had decided that ten was too many for the *Tana* to carry. And so the others, whom I politely named, were forced to rent a dinghy and outboard motor. But then they developed their own program of search, which did not coincide with ours. They wished to investigate, for instance, the north side of the island and look for some golden domes that one of them had dreamed of a few days before, and we wanted to look for the "column" first seen in 1957. Each group wanted Valentine along. Luckily, for us I suppose, the *Tana,* rather than the rented dinghy, appealed to his highly developed sense of comfort.

As I have said, there were ten of us, and probably their names here would be useful. In the white trunks, Margaret Adams, Marguerite Barbrook, Michael and myself. And in the black: Doctor of Psychiatry Lloyd Hotchkiss and his wife, Betty, both thirty-something, I suppose, and from Lexington, Massachusetts, Peter Strello, a member of Lexington's finest, and his wife, Pam—these four were spending their vacations looking for Atlantis; and Mrs. Maud Fennel, a friend of the four, same age, whose husband, evidently, had not been able to come along. And in the middle Dr. Manson Valentine, entomologist, with, as it later developed, a particular interest in beetles.

We had come to love and trust Margaret and Marguerite, instinctively. I think we found each others' drawbacks and idiosyncrasies amusing, endearing (someone once said to me if you like somebody, you like the way they smell) and reassuring. There was, among the four of us, good communication and an excellent distribution of temperament and talent. In short we got along in close quarters without hassles. Margaret had hoped, if not fully expected, that this would be the case with everybody involved with the search. Believing beautifully in this, she happily introduced people to each other like Dolly Levi. And when the mixture didn't take, she was slightly mortified. But I must say that beneath her sometimes overly optimistic, if not downright Pollyannic, exterior, there existed a realism and sense of order that enabled her to choose up sides with the rest of us. She was definitely the genie of the expedition. She believed in its importance and she devoutly wished for its success; but more than that, she had adopted it as a cause. She had invested much time, some money, which didn't matter, and a lot of emotion, which did, into it. And practical woman that she basically is, she was not about to be foiled by the conflicting motives of others. She believed that love and openness would carry herself and the rest of us through to our goals, but when the black magic, the evil eye, and curses began flying, and when it looked as if love alone would not see us through, she took us aside again and instructed us, very sensibly, in the exquisite art of parapsychological self-defense.

Now began the most intense days of the voyage, the five days of expedition, February 23 to 28, 1969. It is easy to oversimplify our attitudes in arriving on Bimini that first morning. Michael, Margaret, and Marguerite were very much excited, especially Margaret, who externalizes every emotion she feels, as she feels it, and so therefore seemed the most excited of the three. Lloyd Hotchkiss, psychiatrist, seemed a bit anxious without his wife. At any rate, he did not seem to be overenjoying himself. For my part, I was quite consciously keeping an open mind. I was lucky enough to sense that I was where I was supposed to be, in time and place, and with the right people, doing the right thing; but in the face of all this optimism, and I thought, overenthusiasm, I felt it necessary to play the good-natured heavy, frivolous but dependable. This choice of roles suited us all. Again, I would say there was good distribution of temperament.

We had our breakfast, and the ladies and Lloyd went up to get hotel rooms. Michael and I napped until just past two. The weather had roughened, as expected (thus the midnight creep from Miami) and we spent the rest of the day discussing our quite vague plans, and walking about the island. Michael and I entertained Margaret and Marguerite for dinner at eight o'clock, Lloyd having retired early to his hotel room. The four of us talked of many things, difficult to recall now. Dr. Valentine had been expected on the afternoon plane from Miami, but he hadn't appeared. The ladies said they would meet the morning plane, just in case. Margaret planned to return by plane to Miami the next afternoon, to collect Lloyd's wife and her three friends, put them up for the night at her house, and then bring them all back the following morning.

The next morning we were up at nine. The M's and Lloyd came aboard at ten for scrambled eggs. Then Marguerite went off to meet the Miami plane, which arrived about eleven o'clock without Valentine. Soon after that, the five of us cast off, under an inconstant sun, and moved out into a quite choppy sea. We had decided to look for a "column" found during an earlier expedition, and photographed by Dr. William Bell of Marion, North Carolina, in 1958. It was reputedly a six-foot column or spire protruding from a double circular gearlike base embedded in the ocean floor. The photographs taken in 1958 showed peculiar emanations of light from the base of the shaft.

It was a very unsuccessful day. The wind and chop was such that we were constantly swung off the sites which we chose, rather randomly, I'm afraid, to explore. Marguerite became ill, though lint-white and prostrate on the cabin couch, she insisted she was not. We had brought with us the bearings from the old expedition, but they seemed impossible to follow. We anchored, rather amateurishly, three times, and snorkeled around, looking down always on a particularly uninteresting, almost barren sandy bottom. The boat, in the changeable winds, would swing around and foul the anchor, and on the third and final site, I was forced to snorkel down and free it, at which exercise, as it turned out, I was not very efficient. Feeling half-drowned, cross, and disorganized, I crawled up into the boat, just in time to realize we were about to lose our 33 foot radio antenna. Michael caught it as it fell, and, as luckily, the securing nut, which had come off, was caught in a deck fitting and had not gone overboard. Things, I thought, were definitely acting against us. Meanwhile, the official bearings having been forgotten, everyone was pointing in different directions, saying I think the column is over there. It was all very desperate and depressing and chaotic. And exercising my right as captain of the vessel, I said, to hell with the column, and brought us all back to Alice Town.

Margaret returned to Miami that afternoon as planned to meet and bring back Lloyd's party. We had Marguerite and Lloyd aboard for a dinner of steak and salad, and afterward an exercise in "regression" suggested by an article in *Orion* magazine that Margaret had read and left on the boat. I can't recall the exact issue or the author. The technique involved was one of semi-hypnosis or suggestion, in which the body and mind are stretched with a series of very simple preliminary questions, and then one is able to go into former lives.

Having made oneself comfortable on a bed or couch, in a dimly lighted, quiet room, eyes closed and covered with a light cloth, one is asked to imagine he is one foot taller through his feet. When that sensation is achieved, mentally, he signals verbally that he has done so; then he is told to return to his normal height. Next, he is told to imagine he is one foot taller through the top of his head. When he says he has done this he is told to shrink again to normal. This process is repeated several times, through the feet and the head, and each successive time the measurement is increased, up to four or five feet, and in between each expansion, the subject is asked to return to normal size.

In the second stage of questions, the subject is told to imagine he is a balloon, and to make his body blow up to twice its normal size; and then to as big as he can make it. Next, he is told to float up in the air in this condition, to about 500 feet above the place he considers home. When the subject indicates he has done this, he is asked to describe any action, particular details, the conditions of light and darkness. He is asked, then, to change the scene from day to night, or vice-versa, depending on which occurs first. When he has changed the scene back and forth four or five times, this question is asked: Who has been changing it from day to night? And the subject will almost always reply, I am.

At this point, the subject is told to remain up in the air, floating as a balloon, and then to slowly let himself come down to the ground, not in the place where his home is necessarily, but any place at all, in another lifetime. He must come down very slowly, and as he feels his feet touching the ground, he must describe them; that is, he must see what kind of footwear, if any, he is wearing, and on what sort of ground or floor he is standing. This is the beginning of the actual regression. Usually, the style of shoes and the kind of floor will describe the time and setting of the regression. The subject is then told to describe the rest of his costume and then his surroundings.

Marguerite and Michael took notes, while Lloyd asked me the prescribed questions. I passed through a rather boring incarnation as a tall clearly American settler with twisted knees, who dies going over a waterfall, to one more interesting: a Lady Catherine something. Cate was a twinkling blonde who entered dancing and progressed from a tête-à-tête with Benjamin Disraeli to a death scene in her boudoir, a death caused by hemorrhaging from the vagina. After Lady Catherine, who lived somewhere named Marley or Marleigh, the name of the house or district, there appears a king, most likely Minoan (which I find fascinating, considering the Thera-Crete-Atlantis theory talked of earlier) in a highly imaginative and intriguing throne room. The letters S A B seem to identify the king or something about him. He has two sons and a wife with four nipples. Since it is a bare-breasted culture, this gives her added power.

Needless to say, we were riveted by these glimpses into the past. Joan Grant had written that "far memory" could be developed by anyone, but having done it, it all seemed a bit too easy. There was actually nothing of hypnosis in the exercises, nor any real need for silence or solemnity once the process had begun. Several times during it, I stopped and sat up to talk about what was happening; and then I would lie down again and resume what was very like watching a movie, as if I had just gotten up to buy some popcorn. At certain times I would be watching myself (though it never looked like me, especially when I was the courtesan, Lady Catherine), or I would actually be inside the person seeing through his eyes. And I would look down and see robes or buckskin, etc. The visualization of the King was the most interesting, because it was the most detailed, the strangest and, I suppose, the splashiest.

After Marguerite and Lloyd left, Michael and I sat talking about it. And I said that I was highly suspicious of the process. I had been trying to develop my imagination for years. Making up stories was my interest and this was, perhaps, little more than cleaned-up fantasy. Michael (first explaining that, as he had not tried it yet, he could not be authoritative) said this did not preclude the possibility that it is through the imagination that we hook into past lives. Indeed, what other function of the brain stands a better chance of tapping the subconscious? But it does presuppose, I said, that the past lives are in there, somewhere, to be tapped, and that they can be tapped at all. Yes, it does, he said, and we went to sleep.

The next morning, Margaret and the rest of the party

not having come yet from Miami, the four of us met again on the boat to put Michael through some regressions. Again, from Michael's journal: "My turn. After breakfast, with Marguerite and Robert taking notes, Lloyd asking the preliminary questions. First stop: grazing land, with white, long-horned cattle, myself as shepherd or tender, in Mu. Very little action, until death by cobra bite. A fat wife and round faced Eskimo-like children. Next stop, a bolting horse which is held for me by two grooms; a knight, with other knights examining a map of England that looks like one of Italy, with small crosses in the surrounding water. In a castle, not very well furnished, then to a jousting match where I merrily lop off someone's head. Last scene is being thrown by same white horse and landing in the mud. Something about Cornwall.

"Stop number three: London about 1914, a bushy Clarence Day sort named Edwards, about 40, who walks out of his frame house at 2157 Rockingham Lane (I have an Essex exchange number) to pick up a copy of the Daily Mail, on it a photo of a large ship sinking, the *Lusitania*. A trip to the ballet where I am bored with Nijinsky. Finally I am hit by a car, feel the impact in my chest and, presumably, die.

"Last stop: I'm fat, female and quite black, with masses of patchwork skirts, in a kitchen, stirring a large pot. A negro midwife, named Evangeline, who is fond of reading of Rebecca in the Bible and has a husband Jacob and a son Joseph. Jacob is a gray haired junkie, and Joseph is the son of a white man named Crockett. I cut umbilical cords with my teeth and have never been more than fifty miles from where I was born. Somewhere between Savannah and Tuskegee. I die in bed."

When we had gotten through all this, Marguerite and Lloyd went off to do some errands, but not before we had discussed the regressions. I was more skeptical than ever and said so. As for the Mu thing, I agreed with everyone else—it was little more than boring, a warm-up for the rest. But the second bit, about the knight reduced me to pure skepticism, and when Michael came up with the initial L on a shield, I nearly burst out laughing. It seemed to me that people are not content with having lived before, they have also to have been major figures in the past—kings, queens, conquerors, famous pirates, etc., including myself, the late, great king of Minoa. And now, here at last we had Sir Lancelot accounted for. The list of people left to have been was getting short. Marguerite told of the figures some of her friends had been in past lives, and then she said the part about England looking like Italy made sense, because Cornwall, mentioned in the regression, had been called the Italy of England. Its cartological similarity to the Italian boot, she said, was famous. This was a clue which Michael insisted he knew nothing about previously, and I believed him.

The third regression was to him the most exciting and important. It was filled with clues—names, addresses, dates—the only difficulty being that it seemed to coincide, chronologically, with the fourth regression, that of the midwife, Evangeline. No matter, we said, and pressed on. Marguerite could not remember, offhand, the exact date of the *Lusitania* affair, though we all thought it had started World War One. And then, recently, a friend of ours went to London and while he was there he sent Michael this card. "There's Rockwell Rd, NW2, Rockhampton Clo. SE27, some Rockhampton Rds, and Rock Hill SE26. Try Rockingham St. SE1. How about Rock Hill? (SE26). For Rockinghill, the number to call is . . ."

In the afternoon, Michael took the dinghy and explored

146

a small buggy island (Pigeon Cay) that yielded nothing just a few hundred yards from the boat in the harbor, and I decided that with all these people coming the *Tana*'s brightwork needed polishing. In mid-afternoon, people began to arrive.

Dr. Manson Valentine arrived at 3:45, along with Margaret, Lloyd's wife, Peter and Pam Strello, and Mrs. Maud Fennel, all from Lexington, down to find Atlantis on their vacation. Valentine had had the flu, which was why he'd not come earlier, and he retired to his hotel room soon after arrival. The rest of us met for dinner that night at Brown's Hotel. There were ten of us, the tenth being Monny, the young British journalist we had met in Miami, who, as Michael says in his journal, "was somewhat dazed by the company." I remember that he left the next morning for Cape Kennedy and that he did not say very much at table. I think he was astounded and that he perhaps lacked what Darwin called cryptic coloration, the ability to adapt one's self to strange situations.

Brown's Hotel is the social center of gravity for the natives of Bimini. The tourist fishermen spend most of their time on their big white boats or in the Big Game Lounge, but the natives gather around Brown's bar every night. Our stay on Bimini coincided with the last part of Adam Clayton Powell's political exile. It was to Brown's that he went to see his adopted constituents, coming over from South Bimini in his boat, *Adam's Fancy*. We saw him several times, and we greeted each other, but I never had the pleasure of a conversation with him. I don't remember whether he was there on this occasion or not. Most likely he was, and it is pleasant to think that Brown's, pound for pound, had a higher energy-level emanation than any other place of its kind for a thousand miles. As Anoush, the Armenian Rug Lady, once said to me, the beautiful people find each other.

Margaret, Marguerite, Monny, Michael and I (the preponderance of M's in this entire thing has always scared me) came into the dining room. Lloyd and his wife, Betty, Peter and Pam Strello, and Maud Fennel were all seated at a large table at the other end of the room. We went over to them and there began a furiously and studiously antic spate of introductions. I believe their reception was designed to put us at our ease.

Ten names were rapidly exchanged, and I found myself sitting between Betty and Maud, with Michael on Maud's left. Across from me sat Peter Strello, who seemed rather likable and benign for a policeman, and who had his right arm in a cast. But before any of us could politely inquire into the story behind that, Betty was asking all of us our sun signs and ascendencies. I told her I was Libra with Scorpio rising. Maud said something about Kenneth Anger and we were off.

Pam, the policeman's wife and a hairdresser, who was sitting opposite Betty, leaned across and asked her if she remembered the dream. Yes, My God, that's right, Betty said, and looked at me with amazement. I arranged my face in an expression of good-natured interest, this having happened early on, and she said, Pam had had a dream about two men coming from Rome, one with a beard and the other a mustache. I believe Margaret had just delivered her little speech about Michael and me dropping everything, art shows, novels, movie careers, leaving Rome and coming down. Pam continued to tell us about the dream and then was very quiet for the rest of the meal, feeling, no doubt, intimidated in the face of something larger than she had imagined.

The food was all right and the conversation a kind of

148

fast, grade-school repartee which was soon replaced with pointed clarifications; one of these was my statement, which they interpreted as a declaration of war, that ten people plus diving gear would not be possible on the *Tana,* and that the ladies, with the exception of course of Margaret and Marguerite, would do better to amuse themselves with scrimshaws while we men searched for Atlantis.

We had our coffee quietly, for all my memory tells me of it, and then we all took a long walk together. The night was very dark and clean and we soon picked up a retinue of the island dogs. As we walked along someone brought up a subject that had been raised at table—the need for a small dinghy, preferably glass-bottomed, and motor, for inshore exploration. Maud announced that if we took her to where such boats were to be found, she would secure the use of one for us. We went on to the Big Game Club, where, I would say, about four million dollars' worth of thirty- to sixty-foot fishing boats and a few larger yachts were moored. The *Tana* lay in the midst of them, holding her own very nicely, and suitable oohs were ahhed by everybody. One of the yachts, a Chris-Craft, I think, had a perfect little dinghy tied off to its stern, which we pointed out to Maud. She nodded her head and went over to the lighted cabin window of the boat and peered inside. I walked away, and the rest of the party followed me. We looked back once to see Maud sitting on the gunnel, crooking her finger through the glass to those aboard. We moved on, and Betty said, She'll get it. We did not see her again until the next morning. There was a proper excuse involved, which I forget, but she had not gotten the dinghy.

It was the following day, Wednesday, February 26, that we found what we found.

We pulled away from the Big Game Club at 10:25, with Margaret, Marguerite, Dr. Valentine, Dr. Lloyd Hotchkiss, Peter Strello, Michael, and myself aboard. It was the perfect day for underwater exploration. The sky was cloudless, the winds were down and southerly, and the water was placid and wonderfully clear.

We had secured the use of a guide and dinghy for the day (whose fifty-dollar fee was paid for by Margaret). The guide's name was Evangelo, a tall, quiet native fisherman who seemed to have a startlingly keen knowledge of the waters around Bimini. Throughout the day he would lead us back and forth across the reefs on the western side of the island, knowing instinctively where the *Tana* could and couldn't go. At times the fathometer showed no more than a foot of water under the keel (which would mean he was leading us through only five feet of water) but we never touched bottom.

We went first to look for the "column," mentioned earlier. Evangelo knew of it, it had been used as a fishing marker for years by some of the Bimini guides, but he said it was covered with sand and had been for a while. We drifted about for a half-hour or so, but did not find it. As far as I know it has never been sighted since the initial discovery in 1958.

Next we moved up to the southern point of North Bimini, just northward of the channel entrance, and anchored to investigate a wreck 150 to 200 feet offshore. This had, really, very little to do with the day's project. We spent about an hour snorkeling in fifteen- or twenty-foot water, diving on some blocks of stone near the wreck, to confirm a previous opinion that they had been the ship's ballast. They had.

And then, led by Evangelo, we sailed northward up the west coast of North Bimini to a point a little beyond a large, four-storied house, on a promontory called Paradise Point, and immediately in front of a gap in a long line of pine trees running along the crest of the island. Bearings taken by Michael indicated a position from which the gap in the tree line lay at 135° S.E., Paradise Point 190°, and the largest of three coral rocks 225° to the S.W. The *Tana* lay anchored perhaps a bit less than three quarters of a mile offshore. Here, Evangelo had said, we would find some interesting rocks and rock formations, which until recently had been covered with tidal sands.

Even from the surface, we could see that the rocks on the bottom had a geometry, and Lloyd and I quickly got into our gear. Valentine, being close to seventy, took a bit more time with his, and Strello helped him. But meanwhile, the two of us jumped in, and saw an amazing thing. We seemed to have anchored above a wide wall or roadbed that stretched in a nearly north-south direction as far as we could see. Immediately we surfaced and told the others. Michael and Strello grabbed snorkels and jumped in. Margaret and Marguerite got into the *Tana*'s dinghy and peered through a glass viewer from the surface. Valentine, meanwhile, was still getting into his scuba gear and readying his underwater camera for pictures. Margaret handed me a waterproofed Instamatic, and I went back down.

The rocks were nearly all rectangular and on a gigantic scale, the largest of them being about 18 or 20 feet long and 10 feet wide. Some were as small as 5 and 6 feet long. All seemed to have a uniform thickness of 2 or 2½ feet. Lloyd followed the rocks southward, and I swam north. Later we estimated the formation to be about 700 yards long. This was borne out by subsequent examinations.

The first impression one had was that this was an unnatural, man-made, monumental construction. I have very little idea of weights, volume and underwater mass, but the stones seemed to me to weigh many tons each. They were fitted, as can be seen from the photographs, into a pavement pattern of right angles. I remember very clearly feeling like an intruder, because the idea that these stones had been set down in perfect order was so strong that the presence of the artisan was still felt. I took some pictures but the camera jammed, so I just floated about, looking around and poking into crevices. There were a good many small and very colorful fish darting back and forth in fast, instinctively reflexive waves, and one had the feeling of being in a very cunningly appointed fish tank, rather as if its owner had been influenced by the picturesque ruins of a Piranesi print.

A useful thing to do, I thought, would be to take a sample, and I went back up to the boat and got a hammer. I managed quite easily to hack a piece from one of the smaller stones. This I brought up and gave to Margaret, who handed it to Valentine. Then, in the hope of finding something smaller, perhaps even an artifact (there had been some talk about finding one) I went between and under some of the bigger stones, digging in the sand. I found nothing except a small, rectangular brick, about ten inches long and four wide, which had a very sharp flange to it and which greatly resembled the bricks Margaret had shown us in Miami. These, it will be recalled, had come from the "temple" off Andros, the one we had read about in the newspaper in Rome. (At the time I did not know that a Mr. Wilfred Smith claimed to have built this "temple" as a sponge or conch kraal little more than thirty or forty years ago.) And so I thought I had found an important link between two important finds. This brick actually may have been one that had fallen from a passing boat in the recent past.

By now, Dr. Valentine had gotten into the water; once down he was quite proficient. We both took some more photographs. Then, as we were running out of air, we went back up into the boat and tried with the others to sort out and assimilate some of the implications of what had been discovered. Valentine speculated that what we had found might have been a Sac Bey, or White Road, such as run across the Yucatán; and alternately, a sea wall, a plaza, or the floor of a huge temple. Michael and I believe, as do a few others, notably Count Pino Turolla, about whom more later, that the rocks formed a sea wall, or dike, upon part of which a temple might have been constructed. Dr. Valentine dated the structure as at least from eight to ten thousand years B.C., or just before the forming of the Florida Straits. This would have been the last time that this part of the ocean floor could have been above sea level. This dating has seemed logical to all the experts who have investigated the wall, primarily because it does not appear to have ever been suitable or useful in any way as an underwater structure. The only differences of opinion have to do with the possibility, if not likelihood, that the wall is a good deal older than ten thousand years.

It seemed that some of the stones had been disturbed (see picture), and Evangelo informed us that after a hurricane in 1926, many had been dredged up and hauled to Miami for use in the reconstruction of a pier or bridge. It might be that most of the huge formation was still covered by sand at that time, and that those handling the stones mistook the ones that were uncovered for beachrock (which is produced when a layer of rock or lava is broken up by movements of the ocean floor. The rock tends usually to break at right angles and therefore sometimes looks unnatural). I had, for months, in fact, the nagging suspicion that somehow that's all the stones were—common beachrock. But this was simply a way of doubting our tremendous luck in finding them. But I think it is very easy to understand how the stones were not discovered years ago. They may well have been discovered many times. But not for what they really were.

A few very important conditions had to be present: first, in order to get an idea of the true size of the wall and its length, one would have to find it during the relatively short period of time when it was uncovered by tidal sands; second, the water would have to be perfectly clear and still, in order to sight it from the surface; and third, one would have to be in the area itself. This sounds rather stupid until you realize that the wall lies in a particularly uninteresting part of the Bimini shore, where next to no swimming is ever done, even closer in to shore, and very little diving. And fourth, and most importantly, one would have to be looking for very strange things in order to exercise the inclination that what one had sighted was odd and unnatural.

It is true that one puts on the suspension of disbelief with one's aqualung when preparing to dive in the ocean, and one is ready, if not hoping, for anything. But is everybody ready to admit that a few partially uncovered rocks, down in the well-charted back-yard depths of Miami, are the as yet still undiscovered artifacts of men who lived ten thousand years ago? Quite frankly, one is not, nor should be. Rocks with rounded edges are a dime a dozen, taken by themselves. It is only when one is lucky enough to come upon a few dozen gross of them, all in a line, that one may, with impunity, begin to believe he may have found something.

We spent the rest of the afternoon snorkeling on and photographing the site. For various reasons, only a few of these pictures came out, and it wasn't until two months later that a really complete photographic study of the wall was made, by Count Pino Turolla of Miami, an underwater expert, archaeologist-explorer. And we are very grateful to him for allowing us to use his pictures in this book.

It had been an exciting day. Suddenly the idea of our having left Rome to search for Atlantis was not so absurd. Whether our sea wall or roadbed was Atlantean was another question, and something that would have to be decided later. But whatever it was, it had been built by man, and not as an underwater structure. It proved the existence of a preclassical culture in an area of the world in which none was ever thought to have existed.

I do not remember now that any of us had particularly important reflections to make about the find. We talked about the likelihood of its being Atlantean, but the implications and significance of it all escaped us for the moment. We had been pleased for months to think of searching for Atlantis, and we had been pleased to stand in the cockpit of the *Tana* that afternoon and look down through twenty-five feet of bright clear water and see the monumentally unnatural evidence of a very ancient civilization. But now, after a few hours of chatter and the barest amounts of intellectual speculation, we were shocked.

Margaret, Marguerite, and Valentine had been through expeditions before, especially Valentine, and there had been many for him. But I suppose that with his diversified interests, he had become used to finding things. Michael and I had never looked for or found anything. And so of course finding these rocks had seemed ridiculously easy. As a child, one had spent more time looking for Easter eggs, and with much less success.

Quite reasonably, Lloyd's wife and Pam Strello were anxious to see the wall, and the next morning they and their husbands followed the *Tana* back out to the site in a small rented skiff. Maud Fennel had to return home and she had left on the morning flight to Miami.

The weather was again perfect for diving. We did a good deal of moving about with the boat, anchoring in various places to get an over-all idea of the wall. It seemed in places to have spurs out to either side, but it was difficult to determine if this was according to the original construction or the result of strong currents and shifts in the ocean floor. It was these spurs that made us think at the time that this might have been a gigantic plaza.

At about two in the afternoon, Margaret spotted a black, square stone with her viewing glass, about three feet square and off a bit by itself on the western side of the wall. Peter Strello and I went down in scuba gear to investigate. It turned out to have a hewn, pillowlike, convex top, very black, and a perfectly flat and white underside. It was Valentine's opinion that this was one of the most important archaeological finds in a hundred years, Atlantis or no. At any rate, we all latched on to the idea of it primarily, I think, because it was much less unwieldy and more man-made looking than the other much bigger stones. It looked like a huge black pillow resting on the sandy bottom, about forty or so feet from the nearest spur of the wall. Strello and I dug around the edges of it and then Peter gestured that we turn it over. Not being used to weights under water and thinking anyway that a solid three foot stone must weigh a ton at least, anywhere but on the moon, and thinking Peter would not be up to his usual effectiveness because of the cast on his right arm, I doubted we could manage it. I was trying to convey all of this to him in underwater shorthand when he wiggled the fingers of his broken arm, got a grip on the rock by its edge and moved it a bit. When the two of us tried together, it flipped over very easily, and I experienced some more of the super-power of aquanauts. As it came to rest on the bottom and the sand settled, we saw its flat, almost perfectly smooth white underside, as if the pillow had been cleft in half. I left him there and went up to the boat to report. I suggested we bring it up and take it back to Miami. The *Tana* has a huge gin pole for hoisting big fish into the stern, and I was sure we could get the rock aboard without too much trouble. Either that or haul it onto the beach. Valentine said to leave it where it was. I went back down to Peter, we flipped it back over to its original position so it could be easily spotted again from the surface, and then, mainly because I thought something dramatic should be done to mark the occasion, I scratched a big A across the top of it. As far as I know it is still where we left it, and we have not heard of anyone having seen it since then.

The next morning Dr. Valentine, Margaret and Marguerite left on Chalk's airline for Miami. The Hotchkiss-Strello group continued to explore for themselves, but we spent the day pulling the *Tana* back into shape; the winds had freshened, and the waters over the sea wall did not have the previous days' clarity. But all of this was an involved rationalization for the fact that with the M's gone the expedition was for us officially ended. We did not see any of the others that day except to loan them some of our underwater gear which they had asked for.

The following morning, which was March 1, Lloyd came

over to ask our plans. We said we would be leaving for Nassau as soon as weather permitted. Margaret had called the night before to say she would be unable to get the plane (which was to be used to get aerial perspectives of the wall and to take polarized pictures of it), that there was a cold front coming and more bad weather, and that someone from Doubleday & Company had come down from Canada to see Valentine about a book he was supposed to write for them, so that he would be tied up in Miami for the weekend. We were, in other words, free to go off whenever we wished. Lloyd said he and his wife and friends would stay on a few more days, looking for other things and investigating the dreams and psychic hints that Betty and Pam had been receiving. After he left, Michael went out to mail some letters and, quite surprisingly, met Valentine and his wife walking along with a group of people, two male and two female. All seemed somewhat at loose ends; the Valentines, slightly embarrassed, were already engaged in the process of privately publicizing the find. Our function had apparently come to its end, and we left early the next day.

Sunday, March 2nd, from Michael's Bimini Journal: "At 9:30 A.M., we happily leave Bimini. The winds are north-westerly and we have a following sea across the Bank. We stop once to investigate what appears to be a circle with a cut-out shape rising in the middle of it. But it is nothing more than a fanciful bit of coral. We have taken the trouble to stop only because we have been so successful at finding things in the last few days. Passing Chub Cay the bridge tachometer, portside, begins to bounce and, below, the engine commences to cough. We baby it, raising New Providence as the full moon appears. We dock in Nassau at seven-thirty, having gone very slowly for much of the afternoon."

It was a palpable pleasure to leave Bimini. Despite our success there, and the excitement and fascination of what we had done, we both disliked the place. The vibrations were bad, and it is not an attractive island. You go back because you happen to love big-game fishing, or because a friend keeps a house there. One has to have compensatory reasons for returning now and then.

Ultimately, I believe the island has a personality. This may be an example of what I talked about earlier, in Water—that I simply don't understand Bimini. But, again, I think it is a female. And as an animate thing, Bimini is not pleased with herself. To me, she is like a lady come on hard times; a ruined princess. She has an inflated, grandiose recollection of her past, and she resents (until she tastes bile in her throat) her present unfortunate, embarrassing circumstances. But what is worse is this: like most self-pitying and fallen women, she has no idea of the valid focus of her past. She remembers her independence, her youth, her beauty, but she is unwilling or unable to tout that for which she should rightly be proud, whatever it may have been—a beautiful love affair, a famous association, some dazzling affair of the mind. She remembers instead that which everyone has had, forgetting all that was unique and strange and indigenous only to her own peculiar court.

And now she produces packets of frivolous old letters, bound up in green ribbons, to show her friends she has had a past and wit; that even her handwriting was once clear and elegant. But she and all about her are oblivious to this fact: that deep in her satchels, at the bottom of her trunks, high in the attic of her mind, are hidden the secrets and complexities of a lost and forgotten world.

II

I believe that, whereas we had all been beautifully prepared, psychicly, to search for Atlantis, none of us was at all equipped to deal with the implications of finding it. Earlier, in Water, I mentioned that I thought it unlikely Atlantis would ever be "found" intellectually, that even a superexpedition like that to Thera, and the overkill documentation of it which followed, could never account for the huge packet of legends that has been built around the central Atlantis theme. And I think that even this early on in the endeavor, it is evident that huge difficulties beset any new Atlantis theory. The world is loathe to take yet another Atlantean possibility seriously (even if they do love to jabber about the subject in a general, astrologically implicated way), and little wonder. Even I, in the middle of it all, would rather talk about our find as being proof, simply, of a preclassical culture in the Bahamas, already important news archaeologically, rather than get into the confusion of claiming that Atlantis has risen. (It is only because Michael and the rest of my colleagues were from the very beginning Cayce-directed that I find it difficult, and narrow-minded, to think of calling them names, now that their strange theories and whims have paid off. It is impossible to dispute the validity of Cayce when you have proof of one of his major prophecies staring you in your scuba-masked face.)

Yet it is still a question of degree. One is drawn up to a stop before the implications of what was found, as one would be at a many-forked crossroad. Since denial of the evidence is ludicrous, one can begin with speculation that our discovery is what is left of an Olmec, or Mayan outpost. (Because of the dates involved, ascertained both by Count Turolla and Dr. Valentine, it is safe to eliminate the Mayan possibility. The Mayan civilization had not yet come into being ten thousand years ago. Most scholars believe rather that the Olmec became what is thought of as Mayan sometime around 250 B.C. This merger seems logical to many people, though the date of it is probably much earlier.

Now the Olmec is considered to be the oldest major cultural group discovered in Middle America, with current radiocarbon dating placing it about 1250 B.C. The only other high culture in the New World that can claim parallel maturity is the Chavín peoples of Peru. The conservatism of these dates (taken from *The New York Times Encyclopedic Almanac, 1970*) is really astounding. To have any private conversations with field archaeologists and serious anthropologists who are not intimidated by the financial investments made by museums (which detest expensive re-evaluation) is to talk more in terms of 20,000 years B.C. as a more suitable date for an already outstandingly cultured man. One of the implications of our discovery then is to push back conservative dating. It proves that a society of men was at work on some sort of construction, ten or fifteen thousand years ago, in which stone blocks weighing tons were being fitted into place with great sophistication. And this construction took place not in the Yucatán, not in Mexico, but in the Bahamas, of all places, on Bimini, an island which, even after two thousand more years, has still not caught on as anything but a place for spirited fishermen and exiled congressmen.

I don't wish to get ahead of myself here. There is much

to say. I am reminded of a device first established in silent movies. Pauline is tied up in a heap on the railroad tracks. Her only chance is Rin-Tin-Tin or Lassie's grandmother, who runs for the Hero up the road. The dog gallops in, twitching and barking madly (though silently), and the Hero somehow realizes his sweetheart needs him.

The dog is incapable of giving a detailed explanation of what has happened to Pauline, and it is unable to suggest ways and means to help her specifically. All it can do is throw a barking fit, and signal, as doggies do, by running four or five feet in one direction repeatedly. But because the Hero is bright, he gets the message.

So Michael and I are the doggies. The best we can do, in our nearly hopeless ineptitude as archaeologists or scientists or anthropologists, is rather hysterically run up and down and make noises, and hope that the hero gets to Pauline in time, or that the master somehow finds the corpse we have dug up in the garden.

The following are excerpts from a synopsis sent to us by Count Pino Turolla of his work with the discovery off Bimini:

"Because of my experience in underwater photography and exploration, and archaeological research in South America, on March 15, 1969, I was asked to join an expedition to investigate and photograph a strange symmetric stone layout on the ocean floor off the west coast of North Bimini Island. This expedition was sponsored by Carter Lord, a young man very much interested in researching the truth of the Cayce predictions. Dr. Manson Valentine, an entomologist with interests in archaeology, his wife Ann, and my wife, Renee, were also part of this group.

"Angelo, a local Bimini fisherman, was our guide in finding the site. On reaching it, I immediately put on my scuba diving gear and dove. The scene was overwhelming. When my feet reached the bottom I was standing over a rectangularly cut stone approximately ten feet by five feet and two and one-half feet thick. The surrounding stones were perfectly matched, some smaller, some bigger but connected to each other like a huge mosaic pavement. I calculated that the width of the site of these square and rectangularly cut stones was at least sixty feet across. The scene was startling because this huge stone lay-out stuck out clearly from the monotonous flatness of the sand covered bottom. The depth varied from between fifteen to thirty-five feet.

"Carter joined me at the bottom and I proceeded to take the photographic record of the site. My conviction from the first moment I saw this gigantic stone work was that this was certainly, without doubt, work done by intelligent beings and not a nature produced phenomenon. Perhaps it was part of a wall construction when the land was above the sea.

"After diving over the site for several hours, Carter and I decided to pull up one of the smaller stones from the bottom for closer examination. To our amazement, this stone, after it was dried in the sun, had a metallic sound when struck. Carl Holm, President of Global Oceanics, who examined this stone block, is of the opinion that it is not a native stone of Bimini or the Bahamas." (It is not immediately obvious that Count Turolla is implying that all the blocks in the stone wall or roadbed are foreign to the Bahamas. The understanding is that the stone brought up was typical of the rest of the stones in everything but size, so it is reasonable to conclude that if this stone was not considered to be indigenous then neither were the rest of them.)

In the next paragraph of his statement, Count Turolla

163

explains a discovery of his own in the same area as ours. Taken together, they make astounding archaeological news:

"On July 12, 1969, Dr. Frances Farrelly, Dr. Edwin Boyle, Jr., Renee and myself were diving off Bimini. During our search of the waters on the west side, we suddenly came upon what appeared to be broken sections of pillars, some embedded in the sea floor in a vertical position, some lying partly covered by the sand, all heavily encrusted with marine life.

"The visible sections of these pillars varied in length between three to five feet and the diameter between two to three feet. Dr. Boyle and I, independently and together, on subsequent trips, found more groups of these pillars on the floor bed. On several occasions I photographed them. On the last trip, November 29, 1969, we were able to secure part of one pillar for closer examination. Subsequent analysis and opinion from experts is that the composition of the sample pillar is not domestic stone from the Bahamian banks or man made material but, rather, *seems to have been carved from natural stone, perhaps from South America.* More investigation is being undertaken now. The photographs included, herewith, are part of the only known series of photographs ever taken of these pillars."

One clarification: Pino explained to us that the pillars were located at intervals, and in groups, along the western, or seaward edge of the wall. Also he noticed that alongside the wall, also at intervals there were carved depressions in the sand, looking like shallow stone wells, for the most part square but greatly filled in; and it was his opinion that the pillars had once stood in these depressions along all or part of the wall.

It will be remembered also that it was Count Turolla's

164

opinion, and the opinion of other experts, that the stone from the wall was not indigenous to the Bahamas. And now, Pino testifies that neither is the pillar stone indigenous. He has since told us that the stone seems to come from the Andes Mountains. Valentine, meanwhile, maintains the possibility that before the forming of the Straits of Florida, a land bridge connected what is now the Bahamas with South America. It may be that this stone, all of it, and the pillars, were trucked overland to the Bimini site. Or, according to Count Turolla, it is quite possible that the Andes range extended, on this land bridge, all the way up to the Bahamas, so that what is not now indigenous to the area, may have been fifteen thousand years ago, or more.

But if the Andes did not come further north in ancient times, then it must be said that the builders of the wall and pillars went to great trouble to construct it. And Michael reasons that stone would have been brought such a great distance (over 1000 miles) only if it was considered particularly special. He believes, because of this, that we perhaps found, among other things, the temple of Poseidia, mentioned in the Cayce readings. He suggests that the stone was sacred and came from a sacred place.

I, on the other hand, believe that the Andes did indeed extend up into the Caribbean and beyond, and that the stone was quarried from comparatively close by. I think the pillars (of which forty-four have been found so far by Count Turolla) may have been either mooring posts along the sea wall, or part of a temple (perhaps of Poseidia) that was built near or on top of it.

The developments, since returning from the trip, and even since we began writing this book, have been fascinating. Not only did Count Turolla find forty-four pillars (he believes many more are buried beneath the sand), but he has also discovered three other sections of wall. One lies just south of the section we found, off North Bimini, and is about 80 yards long. The other two lie off South Bimini, and are about 350 and 50 yards long respectively. What is particularly astounding is that the last section, of 50 yards, seems to turn eastward around the southern tip of South Bimini. And it is Pino's opinion that the wall may run in a circle all the way around the two islands. If this is true then the predictions of Edgar Cayce have to be taken very seriously indeed. Let us suppose that a small continent did exist in the Bahama region, and that due to the rise of the sea, or the subsidence of the land itself, that the continent was broken up into islands. It would be logical, if this happened, for the surviving inhabitants to converge on the island with the highest point above sea-level, and to build a protective wall around it. Such a feat would be comparable to the construction of the Great Wall of China or the Pyramids, if you take into account that its usefulness as a dike would mean it had to have been built at least ten, and more likely fifteen thousand years ago. Here the people lived until the dike was no longer effective. And then, finally, the inexorable sea consumed them or drove them from their land. Both Plato and Cayce put this date at about 9500 B.C., which is compatible with the date which all experts who have seen the wall have given it. Now unless one is determined to hang all of one's coats in the single, cramped cloakroom of mere coincidence, one has got to admit that Cayce's prediction about Bimini has, like so much else he said, been proven relevant. And one has got to decide how much credit and credence to give the prediction now that so much has come of it. I believe, skeptic that I am, that if a man finds a

needle in the haystack, his companions should have the grace
and good manners to admit that it was indeed the needle that
had been lost.

We have been told that in a few weeks time an announce-
ment will be made concerning plans for the excavation of
the wall, to determine how many layers it has (two have been
found so far), how long it actually is, and if, most importantly,
it really goes around the two islands of Bimini. Count Turolla
and Carl Holm, President of Global Oceanics, have been
forming an agreement with a prominent American industrial-
ist who has extensive holdings in the Bahamas. Together with
this man, they are obtaining excavation rights and funds.

The situation is in its purest state right now. A few people
know of the find, and they believe in it. Fewer still have
been down to see it, and they are caught up with its implications. Now begins the rather seedy business of populari-
zation, during which all shades of gray and pearl must be
sacrificed to the cold, sensational starkness of black and white.
It must now become a public thing, and what had been important to us, and personal, must be generalized and sur-
rendered to people at large. But this is, after all, a consequence of our involvement. One cannot slap the hindquarters
of the messenger's horse without expecting it to go galloping
off down the road to spread the news in town.

We left the sea wall, then, not very long after we found it.
For two more months we lingered in the Bahamas, and then,
having been unable to do any more in the way of group
exploration of the Bimini site, we returned up the Waterway
to Brielle, New Jersey, arriving there May 3.

Some few days after our return, we were asked to lunch

by an editor who had read a New York *Times* article about us, and was interested in our trip. A few days later we were asked to write a nonfiction account of it by that same editor.

And we have and this is it.

New York
February 1970